California Eastern District

COURT AND CHAMBERS PRACTICE MANUAL

DISTRICT COURT
Selected General Orders

INDIVIDUAL JUDGES
Procedures and Practices
Scheduling Information
Chambers and Biographical Information

Mid-2012 Edition

Compiled by Practicing Attorneys
Meliora Law

This publication is created to provide accurate and authoritative information concerning
the subject matter covered. It is sold with the understanding that the publisher is not
engaged in rendering legal or other professional advice. If legal or other expert
advice is required, the services of a competent professional should be sought.

Printed and bound in the United States of America.
ISBN: 978-0-9838302-2-1

Comments and corrections may be sent to comments@melioralaw.com. Although
the publisher has made every effort to ensure the accuracy of information contained
in this publication, it cannot assume liability for inadvertent errors.

Meliora Law LLC
19250 Stevens Creek Boulevard, Suite 100
Cupertino, CA 94015
www.melioralaw.com

PUBLISHER'S PREFACE

The information contained herein are current as received through March 2012.

THE PUBLISHER

March 2012

TABLE OF CONTENTS

PART I

District Court
Selected General Orders

I.   <u>General Orders</u>
    A.   <u>*General Order No. 515*</u>

GENERAL ORDER NO. 515

IN RE: RECUSAL WHEN FORMER JUDGE APPEARS AS COUNSEL

    The District Judges of the Eastern District of California have met and have decided the issue of recusal of its judges when a former Eastern District judge (either district or magistrate) appears as counsel. The Court will follow the guidelines provided by the United States Federal Courts Committee on Codes of Conduct, Advisory Opinion No. 70, which in part states: "The Committee recommends that courts announce a policy that for a fixed period after the retirement or resignation of a colleague, judges recuse themselves in any case in which the former colleague appears as counsel." This general recusal will last for a one year period from the date that the former judge left the Court.

    IT IS SO ORDERED.

DATED: _____   FOR THE COURT:

                                      _____/s/_____

                                      ANTHONY W. ISHII, Chief Judge
                                      Eastern District of California

B.   *General Order No. 493*

GENERAL ORDER NO. 493
IN RE: ADOPTION OF AMENDED JURY SELECTION PLAN

April 26, 2010, the Judges of the Eastern District of California adopted General Order No. 491, Adoption of Amended Jury Selection Plan (attached), pending approval by the Judicial Council of the Ninth Circuit.

June 24, 2010, the Judicial Council for the Ninth Circuit approved the Eastern District of California's Amended Jury Selection Plan.

IT IS HEREBY ORDERED that the Amended Jury Selection Plan is adopted and becomes effective this date.

DATED: June 25, 2010.   FOR THE COURT:

                                     _____/s/_____
                                     ANTHONY W. ISHII, Chief Judge
                                     Eastern District of California

UNITED STATES DISTRICT COURT
Eastern District of California

JUROR MANAGEMENT PLAN

(Adopted by the Court April 7, 2010; Revised June 14, 2010)
ANTHONY W. ISHII
CHIEF JUDGE

CHAPTER ONE
General Matters

Section 1.01   **Authority**
The United States District Court for the Eastern District of California adopts this Juror Management Plan in accordance with the provisions of the Jury Selection and Service Act of 1968 (Public Law 90-274), as amended and codified in 28 U.S.C. § 1861 *et seq.*

Section 1.02   **Application**
This Plan will take effect after approval by a reviewing panel of the United States Court of Appeals for the Ninth Circuit pursuant to 28 U.S.C. § 1863(a). The prior Jury Plan will be superseded as of the effective date of this revised Plan.

Section 1.03   **Juror Management Defined**
For purposes of this Plan, the phrase *juror management* will be deemed to include all activities associated with the master and qualified jury wheels relating to the selection, qualification, and service of grand and petit jurors.

Section 1.04   **Policy**
It is the policy of the Court that all litigants in this Court, entitled to trial by jury, shall have the right to grand and petit juries selected at random from a fair cross section of the community in the district or division in which the Court convenes, and that all U.S. Citizens residing within the District shall have the opportunity to be considered for service on grand and petit juries, and shall have an obligation to serve as jurors when summoned for that purpose. No U.S. Citizen shall be excluded from service as a grand or petit juror because of race, color, religion, sex, national origin, or economic status.

Section 1.05   **Management Responsibilities**
In accordance with 28 U.S.C. § 1863(b)(1), the Clerk of Court will manage the juror management process under the supervision and control of the Chief Judge. The term "Chief Judge" shall mean the Chief Judge of this District, or any supervising judge appointed by the Chief Judge.

(a) Approved Management Methods: The Court finds that electronic data processing methods can be advantageously used for managing this Plan. Therefore, a properly programmed electronic data processing system or a combination system employing both manual and electronic machine methods, may, at the Clerk's option after consultation with the Chief Judge, be used for all randomized drawings and to perform other clerical and record-keeping jury functions.

In the event of an emergency, computer malfunction, or any overt or obvious deviation from this Plan caused by automation, the Clerk, with the approval of the Chief Judge, shall manually, or by alternative electronic methods, proceed from the last step correctly implemented.

Section 1.06 **Delegation of the Clerk's Management Responsibilities**
In accordance with 28 U.S.C. §§ 1863(b)(1) and 1869(a), the Clerk of Court may delegate responsibility for the day-to-day operation of the jury management process to any authorized deputy clerk, or to any non-court person or agency authorized pursuant to Section 1.10 below.

Section 1.07 **Jury Management Divisions** (*See* 28 U.S.C. § 1869(e) and Local Rule 120)
To facilitate juror management activities, the Clerk is directed to align the Eastern District of California's counties into the following jury management divisions:

(a) **<u>SACRAMENTO DIVISION</u>**: consisting of the counties of Siskiyou, Modoc, Trinity, Shasta, Lassen, Tehama, Plumas, Glenn, Butte, Colusa, Sutter, Yuba, Sierra, Nevada, Yolo, Placer, El Dorado, Solano, Sacramento, Amador, Alpine, San Joaquin, and Mono.

(b) **<u>FRESNO DIVISION</u>**: consisting of the counties of Merced, Mariposa, Madera, Fresno, Inyo, Kings, Tulare, Kern, Calaveras, Stanislaus, and Tuolumne.

Jurors will be selected for service from a single division or from a combination of divisions as the Chief Judge may from time to time direct. The provisions of this Plan apply to both divisions in the District, unless specifically indicated to the contrary.

Section 1.08 **Emptying and Refilling the Master Jury Wheels**
The Clerk of Court shall create and maintain a master jury wheel for each of the divisions within the District. In accordance with 28 U.S.C. § 1863(b)(4), the Clerk is directed to empty and refill the master jury wheels by October 1st each year, with a total number as may be deemed sufficient for a period of one (1) year. The Chief Judge may grant additional time to empty and refill the master jury wheels as needed.

Section 1.09 **Emptying and Refilling the Qualified Jury Wheels**
When the master wheels are emptied, the existing qualified wheels will continue to be used until the Clerk determines that an adequate number of persons from the new master wheels have been qualified. At that time, the old

qualified wheels will be emptied and new qualified wheels created. Jurors from previous qualified jury wheels may serve at the same time with jurors selected from later qualified jury wheels.

Section 1.10   **Use of Non-Court Personnel**
The Clerk may use the services of non-court personnel to assist in the juror management process. For purposes of this plan, the phrase "*non-court personnel*" may include, but is not limited to:

(a) County or State of California officials, and their employees or agents, who are responsible for custody and maintenance of the source lists identified in Section 2.01 of this Plan.

(b) Owners, employees, operators and/or agents of computer or data processing centers, bar-coding facilities, mail handling centers, document reproduction facilities, and optical scanning facilities, whose services are requested or employed by the Clerk to support the juror management Process.

(c) Other non-court administrative or clerical persons whose services are requested or employed by the Clerk to select, process, and/or mail the various documents and records involved in the juror management Process.

Section 1.11   **Method and Manner for the Random Selection of Jurors**
The randomized selection procedures set forth in this Plan ensure that the names chosen will represent all segments of the source file from which drawn, that the mathematical odds of any single name being picked are substantially equal, and that the possibility of human discretion or choice affecting the selection of any individual's name is eliminated.

(a) Purely Randomized Process: At the Clerk's option, and after consultation with the Chief Judge, the selection of names from the complete source list databases in electronic media for the master jury wheels may be accomplished by a purely randomized process through a properly programmed electronic data processing system. Similarly, at the option of the Clerk and after consultation with the Chief Judge, a properly programmed electronic data processing system for pure randomized selection may be used to select names from the master wheel to determine qualification for jury service, from the qualified wheel for summoning persons to serve as grand or petit jurors, from the pool of jurors to serve as a panel, and from the panel of jurors to serve as a jury. Such random selections of names from the source lists for inclusion in the master wheels by data computer personnel must ensure that each county within the jury division is substantially proportionally represented in the master jury wheel in accordance with 28 U.S.C. § 1863(b)(3). The purely randomized selection procedure may be used for all drawings. (*See* Section 2.03 herein for the procedures to ensure proper proportional county representation in the divisional master jury wheels.)

(1) The method and manner of purely randomized selection shall be as

follows:

(i) Determining a "Quotient"

The Clerk shall make the systematic randomized selection by taking the total number of names available for selection and dividing that number by the number of names needed for the master wheel. The number obtained will be the "quotient."

(ii) Determining a "Starting Number"

After determining the "quotient," the Clerk shall establish a "starting number." This number will be the first name to be selected. The "starting number" will be manually drawn by lot beginning with the number <u>one</u> and ending with the same number as the "quotient." As an example of how both the "starting number" and the "quotient" are used, if we suppose the "quotient" to be "100" and the "starting number" to be "12," the first name chosen would be the 12th name on the list, the second name would be the 112th, *etc.*, and continued in the same manner to the end of the list.

CHAPTER TWO
Source Lists, Initial Random Selection, and the Master Jury Wheel

Section 2.01 **Source Lists** (*See* 28 U.S.C. §§ 1861 and 1863(b)(2) and (3))
Voter Registration Lists: The Court finds that California county voter registration lists represent a fair cross section of the citizens residing within the communities in the Eastern District of California.

State of California, Department of Motor Vehicle Records: To facilitate broadening the source from which the names of petit and grand jurors shall be selected at random in the Fresno Division, State of California, Department of Motor Vehicles records will be used from all counties within the Fresno Division to augment names from which petit and grand jurors shall be selected. Names of petit and grand jurors, as supplemented by the State of California Department of Motor Vehicle Records selected at random, shall be included in the overall source of prospective jurors in the Fresno Division and processed in accordance with the remaining requirements for initial selection of names for the master wheel method and in the manner of random selection as prescribed in the Articles of the existing Amended Jury Selection Plan of the Eastern District of California, to be applied and implemented in the Fresno Division. The use of the State of California Department of Motor Vehicle Records to augment the master jury wheel in the Fresno Division shall continue in force and effect for such a period of time as shall be determined by the judges of this court.

Section 2.02 **Size of the Master Jury Wheels** (*See* 28 U.S.C. § 1863(b)(4))
(a) Sacramento Division: The names of all persons randomly selected from the voter registration records of the counties in the division shall be placed in

the master jury wheel for that division.

(b) Fresno Division: The names of all persons randomly selected from the voter registration records of the counties in the division and the names of all persons randomly selected from the State of California, Department of Motor Vehicle Records, shall be placed in the master jury wheel for that division. These two lists shall be merged and duplicate records purged. The Court takes notice that when two or more source lists are used, one person's name may appear more than once. The Clerk will, either manually or through automated systems, eliminate as reasonably as possible such duplications before any selection procedures begin.

(c) Pursuant to 28 U.S.C. § 1863 (b)(4) of the Act, the minimum number of names to be placed in the master jury wheels shall be at least one-half of one percent of the total number of names on all county voter registration records.

(d) The Chief Judge may order additional names to be placed in the master jury wheels from time to time as necessary.

Section 2.03 **Substantial Proportional Representation and the Master Jury Wheels**
In accordance with 28 U.S.C. § 1863(b)(3), the Clerk shall determine the number of records needed in the master wheel. The number of names drawn from each county shall be substantially in the same proportion to the total number drawn from all counties within the division. In the Sacramento Division, the proportion shall be substantially the same as the number of names on that county's voter registration records. In the Fresno Division, the proportion shall be substantially the same as the voter registration records combined with the State of California Department of Motor Vehicle records.

Section 2.04 **Filling the Master Jury Wheels**
After first determining the total number of names needed for the master wheel and then the proportionate share of names to be drawn from either the voter registration record of each particular county or a combination of the voter registration record and the State of California Department of Motor Vehicle Records, the Clerk shall proceed, either manually or through a combination of manual and computer methods, to make the initial selection of names from the record of each county.

CHAPTER THREE
Drawing Names from the Master Jury Wheel, Juror Qualification, and the Qualified Jury Wheel

Section 3.01 **Drawing Names from the Master Jury Wheel**
A general notice shall be posted in the Clerk's Office and on the Court's website that explains the process by which names are randomly and periodically drawn from the wheel.

The Clerk, either all at once or at periodic intervals, shall draw at random from the master jury wheels the names of as many persons as may be required to maintain an adequate number of names in the qualified jury wheels. The number of names to be drawn shall be determined by the Clerk based upon anticipated juror needs by the Court plus a margin of extra names sufficient to compensate for the estimated number that will turn out to be unavailable or ineligible.

At the option of the Clerk and after consultation with the court, a properly programmed electronic data processing system for pure randomized selection may be used to select names from the master wheel to determine qualification for jury service, and from the qualified wheel for summoning persons to serve as grand or petit jurors. Such random selections of names from the source list for inclusion in the master wheel by data computer personnel must insure that each county within the jury division is substantially proportionally represented in the master jury wheel in accordance with 28 U.S.C. § 1863 (b)(3). The selections of names from the source list, the master wheel, and the qualified wheel must also insure that the mathematical odds of any single name being picked are substantially equal.

Section 3.02   Mailing Juror Qualification Questionnaires

The juror qualification form prescribed by the Administrative Office of the United States Courts and approved by the Judicial Conference of the United States shall be used.

The Clerk will mail a juror qualification questionnaire to every person randomly selected pursuant to Section 3.01 of this plan (28 U.S.C. § 1864(a)). The juror qualification questionnaire is accompanied by instructions to fill out and return the form, duly signed and sworn, to the Clerk, either by regular mail or through the Court's internet website, within ten (10) days.

Section 3.03   Failure to Return a Juror Qualification Questionnaire

If a person fails to return a completed juror qualification questionnaire, the Clerk may note the failure in the juror's record. Upon Order of the Court, the Clerk thereafter may pursue such matter in accordance with the provisions of 28 U.S.C. § 1864(a) of the Act. No juror fees or costs for this appearance shall be paid, unless otherwise ordered by the Court.

Section 3.04   Determining Juror Qualification Status

The Chief Judge or designated judge, on their own initiative, or upon recommendation of the Clerk, shall determine solely on the basis of information provided on the juror qualification form and other competent evidence, whether a person is unqualified for, or exempt, or to be excused from jury service. The Clerk shall, by manual or computer means, enter this determination in the space provided on the juror qualification form. (28 U.S.C. § 1865(a)). The Clerk shall enter such determination on the juror qualification form or juror records in the database in the master jury wheel.

(a) Disqualification from Jury Service: In accordance with 28 U.S.C. § 1865(b), any person shall be deemed qualified to serve on grand and petit juries in this District unless such person:

(1) Is not a citizen of the United States, eighteen (18) years of age who has resided within the judicial district for one year;

(2) Is unable to read, write and understand the English language with a degree of proficiency sufficient to fill out satisfactorily the juror qualification form;

(3) Is unable to speak the English language;

(4) Is incapable, by reason of mental or physical infirmity, to render satisfactory jury service; or

(5) Has a charge pending against him for the commission of, or has been convicted in a State of Federal Court of record of, a crime punishable by imprisonment for more than one year and his civil rights have not been restored.

(b) Exemption from Jury Service: In accordance with 28 U.S.C. § 1863(b)(6), the following persons are barred from jury service on the grounds that they are exempt:

(1) Members in active service in the Armed Forces of the United States;

(2) Members of the fire or police departments of any state, district, territory, possession, or subdivision thereof; and

(3) Public officers in the executive, legislative, or judicial branches of the Government of the United States, or any state, district, territory, possession or subdivision thereof, who are actively engaged in the performance of their official duties. A "public officer" shall mean a person who is elected to public office or who is directly appointed by a person elected to public office.

(c) Excuses From Jury Service on Individual Request

(1) Permanent Excuse: In accordance with 28 U.S.C. § 1863(b)(5)(A) and (B), the Court finds that jury service by members of the following occupational classes or groups of persons would entail undue hardship or extreme inconvenience to the members thereof, and the excuse of such members would not be inconsistent with §§ 1861 and 1862 of 28 U.S.C., and shall be granted upon individual written request to those:

(1) Over seventy (70) years of age;

(2) persons who have, within the past two years, served as a federal grand or petit juror;

(3) Volunteer safety personnel, specifically individuals serving a public agency in an official capacity, without compensation,

as firefighters or members of a rescue squad or ambulance crew.

(2) Temporary Excuse: In addition to the members of groups and occupational classes subject to excuse from jury service on individual request, any person summoned for jury service may, upon written request, be excused by the Court, or by the Clerk of the Court, upon a showing of undue hardship or extreme inconvenience, for such period as the Court deems necessary, at the conclusion of which such person shall be notified again for jury service within a reasonable time or as the Court may direct. The name of such person shall be reinserted into the qualified jury wheel of the Court.

(1) Undue hardship or extreme inconvenience: as a basis for excuse from immediate jury service under this section shall mean great distance, either in miles or travel time, from the place of holding court, grave illness in the family or any other emergency which outweighs in immediacy and urgency the obligation to serve as a juror when summoned, or any other factor which the Court determines to constitute an undue hardship or to create an extreme inconvenience to the juror; and in addition, in situations where it is anticipated that a trial or grand jury proceeding may require more than thirty (30) days of service, the court may consider, as a further basis for temporary excuse, severe economic hardship to an employer which would result from the absence of a key employee during the period of such service.

Section 3.05   **Qualified Jury Wheels**

The Clerk shall maintain separate qualified jury wheels or devices similar in purpose and function for each division, and shall place in the wheels the names of all persons drawn from the master wheels and not disqualified, exempt or excused pursuant to this Plan. The Clerk shall insure at all times an adequate number of names are maintained in each wheel. The Clerk may maintain these wheels by using an automated system.

CHAPTER FOUR
Selection of Grand and Petit Jurors

Section 4.01   **Selection and Impanelment of Grand and Petit Jurors** (*See* 28 U.S.C. § 1866(a))

From time to time, the clerk shall draw at random from the qualified jury wheel such number of names of persons as may be required for assignment to grand and petit jury panels. The clerk shall post a general notice for public review in the clerk's office and on the court's website explaining the process by which names are periodically and randomly drawn.

Section 4.02   **Summoning Grand and/or Petit Jurors** (*See* 28 U.S.C. § 1866(b))
Upon Court Order, the Clerk shall randomly select, by manual or computer means, from the designated qualified jury wheel the designated number of persons to be summoned for a specific date. Names of persons summoned and appearing for service may be considered as a petit jury pool, from which separate trial panels will be randomly selected by lot. Pooling of jurors, staggered trial starts and multiple voir dire may be used in the assignment of jurors to petit jury panels. The Clerk shall prepare for the Court and counsel a separate list of names of persons assigned to each petit jury panel. Jurors shall complete and return their summons information sheets either by regular mail or through the Court's internet site.

The names of trial jurors may be released to the parties, the public, or the press at the conclusion of a trial (civil or criminal) only upon leave of the court. All requests for release of juror names must be made in writing to the presiding trial judge.

Section 4.03   **Unanticipated Shortage of Jurors** (*See* 28 U.S.C. § 1866(f))
When there is an unanticipated shortage of available petit jurors drawn from the qualified jury wheels, the Chief Judge or designated judge may require the United States Marshal to summon a sufficient number of additional petit jurors. These jurors will be selected at random, in a manner ordered by the Court, consistent with 28 U.S.C. § 1862.

Section 4.04   **Petit Jury Term**
In any two-year period, no person shall be required to:

(a) serve or attend court for prospective service as a petit juror for a total of more than thirty (30) days, except when necessary to complete service in a particular case, or

(b) serve as both a grand and petit juror.

A petit juror required to attend more than ten days in hearing one case may be paid, in the discretion of the trial judge, an additional fee, not exceeding the limit set forth by statute, for each day in excess of ten days on which the juror is required to hear such case.

A petit juror required to attend more than ten days of actual service may be paid, in the discretion of the judge, the appropriate fees at the end of the first ten days and at the end of every ten days of service thereafter.

The judge may order certification of additional attendance fees to be made effective commencing on the first day of extended service, without reference to the date of such certification.

Petit jurors appearing in the United States District Court for the Eastern District of California may, upon completion of their service, be released from further jury service obligations for a period of not less than two years. The Court reserves the right to modify the provisions of this petit jury policy when the interests of justice so require.

Section 4.05   **Disclosure of Petit Juror Information**
(a) To Attorneys and Parties: When the Clerk has assigned a venire panel to a particular trial, the list of names so assigned shall be furnished to the attorneys for the parties and any parties appearing *pro se* in said trial at the beginning of jury selection, unless otherwise ordered by the trial judge. Notwithstanding this general policy, any trial judge may order the Clerk to keep jurors names confidential in any case where the interests of justice so require.

(b) To the Public and the Media: The names and information relating to any prospective or sitting petit jurors shall not be disclosed to the public or media outside open court, except upon order of the Court.

Applications for disclosure of petit juror names or information to the media or public must be made by motion (with a memorandum of authorities) to the presiding trial judge. The presiding trial judge may order the Clerk to keep the jurors' names confidential in any case where the interests of justice so require.

Section 4.06   **Grand Jury Impanelment** (*See* 28 U.S.C. § 1863(b)(8))
From time to time as grand juries are required, the Court shall order the random drawing from each division's qualified wheel the names of persons as may be required for assignment to the grand jury panels. The total number of grand jurors to be summoned shall be based on a pro-rata share of the total number of persons on the voter registration record of each division as compared to the total number of persons on the voter registration records of all divisions. Special grand juries shall be selected in the same manner as regular grand juries.

> **(a) Divisional Grand Juries:** If a grand jury is to be impaneled for service in a division only, the Clerk shall draw at random from the qualified wheel of that division such number of prospective grand jurors as the Chief Judge may direct.

Section 4.07   **Term of Regular Grand Jury**
Each grand jury shall serve until discharged by the Chief Judge, but no regular grand jury shall serve more than 18 months unless the Court extends the service of the grand jury upon a determination that such extension is in the public interest, in accordance with Rule 6(g) of the Federal Rules of Criminal Procedure.

Section 4.08   **Term of Special Grand Jury**
Each Special Grand Jury as defined in 18 U.S.C. § 3331, shall serve for a term of 18 months unless an order for its discharge or an extension of its term is entered by the Court in accordance with Sections 3331 or 3333 of 18 U.S.C.

Section 4.09   **Alternate Grand Jurors**
The Court may direct that alternate grand jurors be selected at the same time a grand jury is selected. Alternate grand jurors, in the order in which they

were selected, may thereafter be impaneled to replace excused grand jurors. Alternate grand jurors shall be drawn in the same manner and shall have the same qualifications as the regular grand jurors, and if impaneled, shall be subject to the same challenges, shall take the same oath, and shall have the same authority as the regular grand jurors.

Section 4.10   **Disclosure of Grand Juror Information** (*See* 28 U.S.C. § 1863(b)(7))

Except as authorized by written order of the court, the names and information relating to any summoned or serving grand juror or grand jury panel will be confidential and not disclosed to any litigant or member of the public. Applications for disclosure of grand juror information must be made by motion (with a memorandum of authorities) to the Chief Judge and must show exceptional and compelling circumstances why disclosure should be allowed.

CHAPTER FIVE
Exclusion or Excuse from Jury Service

Section 5.01   **Exclusion or Excuse from Jury Service** (28 U.S.C. § 1866(c))

Except as provided elsewhere in this Plan, no person or class of persons shall be disqualified, excluded, excused, or exempted from service as jurors; provided, however, that any person summoned for jury service may be:

(a) Excluded by the court on the grounds that such person may be unable to render impartial jury service or that his service as a juror would be likely to disrupt the proceedings;

(b) Excluded upon peremptory challenge as provided by law;

(c) Excluded pursuant to the procedure specified by law upon a challenge by any party for good cause shown;

(d) Excluded upon determination of the court, after hearing in open court, that service as a juror would be likely to threaten the secrecy of the proceedings, or otherwise adversely affect the integrity of jury deliberations, and that exclusion of such person will not be inconsistent with the policy stated in 28 U.S.C. §§ 1861 and 1862.

Section 5.02   **Jury Service Limit**

In any two (2) year period, no person shall be required to:

(a) serve or attend court for prospective service as a petit juror for a total of more than thirty (30) days, except when necessary to complete service in a particular case, or

(b) serve on more than one grand jury, or

(c) serve as both a grand and petit juror.

Section 5.03   Permanent Exclusion or Excuse from Jury Service

Whenever a person is permanently excluded or excused from jury service under this Chapter, the Clerk shall note the same on a record card, the questionnaire, and in the qualified jury wheel.

CHAPTER SIX
Disclosure and Retention of Jury Selection Records

Section 6.01   Release of Jury Plan Information

The clerk is authorized to provide a copy of this Juror Management Plan to any person requesting information about the juror management process, and may post the Plan to the court's public website. All other requests for information about the juror management process must be submitted in writing (with a memorandum of authorities) to the Clerk of Court, who will confer with the Chief Judge prior to releasing any information.

Section 6.02   Release of Juror Records (*See* 28 U.S.C. § 1867(f))

The contents of records and papers used in the juror management process will not be disclosed, except upon written order of the court. Applications for disclosure of juror management records must be made by motion (with a memorandum of authorities) to the Chief Judge and must show exceptional and compelling circumstances why disclosure should be allowed.

Section 6.03   Retention of Juror Records (*See* 28 U.S.C. § 1868)

The clerk will keep all records and papers relating to the juror management process for four years following the emptying and refilling of the master jury wheels and the completion of service of all jurors selected from those master jury wheels, or for such longer periods of time as the Court may require. Such records may then be destroyed, providing the means used ensures the privacy of their Contents.

Section 6.04   Request to Inspect Jury Wheel Records (*See* 28 U.S.C. § 1868)

Applications to inspect juror management records to determine the validity of the selection of any jury must be made by motion (with a memorandum of authorities) to the Chief Judge, and must show exceptional and compelling circumstances why disclosure should be allowed.

ADOPTED with the consent of the Court, the 7th day of April 2010 and revised this 14th day of June 2010.

/s/
Anthony W. Ishii
Chief Judge

C. *General Order No. 466*

GENERAL ORDER NO. 466

AUTHORIZATION FOR THE UNITED STATES PROBATION OFFICE TO DISCLOSE CERTAIN PRESENTENCE REPORTS AND STATEMENTS OF REASON TO THE UNITED STATES ATTORNEY AND FEDERAL DEFENDER

It is hereby ORDERED that, pursuant to Local Criminal Rule 32-460(b), because of the need to efficiently process motions to reduce crack cocaine sentences under 18 U.S.C. § 3582(c)(2), the United States Probation Office is hereby authorized to disclose to the United States Attorney's Office and the Federal Defender's Office the presentence report and statement of reasons of any defendant who might be eligible for a reduction of sentence under the United States Sentencing Commission's policy statement promulgated on December 11, 2007.

IT IS SO ORDERED.

DATED: January 15, 2008   FOR THE COURT:

                                            _____/s/_____
                                            GARLAND E. BURRELL, JR.
                                            Chief United States District Judge

D.   *General Order No. 421*

GENERAL ORDER NO. 421
COMPLIANCE WITH 28 U.S.C. § 994(w)(1)

This General Order of the Eastern District of California is intended to constitute compliance with Section 994(w)(1) of Title 28 as amended effective May 1, 2003.

The United States Probation Department of this District shall submit to the United States Sentencing Commission ("Sentencing Commission" or "Commission") within 30 days of the entry of judgment in every criminal case the following materials:

(A)   the judgment and commitment order;

(B)   the statement of reasons for the sentence imposed (which shall include the reason for any departure from the otherwise applicable guideline range);

(C)   all plea agreements including agreements filed under seal which shall be accompanied by the court order sealing the agreement;

(D)   all indictments, superseding indictments, informations and superseding informations filed in the action from the inception of the action; and

(E)   the presentence report.

It is the practice of this District that the presentence reports include the offense or offenses upon which the sentence is imposed, the age, race, and sex of the offender and all information regarding factors made relevant by the guidelines. The report shall continue to include this information.

The court finds that the above materials contain all of the information required by Section 994(w)(1) sufficient to constitute the written report until such time as the Commission instructs otherwise.

Any sealed materials required to be submitted to the Commission shall be accompanied by the issuing court's sealing order.

This order is intended to meet the requirement that the Chief Judge of this District ensure compliance with Section 994(w)(1) of Title 28 as amended effective May 1, 2003, until further instruction by the Sentencing Commission.

IT IS SO ORDERED.

DATED: September 25, 2003   FOR THE COURT:

                                                  _____/s/_____
                                                  DAVID F. LEVI
                                                  Chief Judge
                                                  Eastern District of California

E.   *General Order No. 415*

GENERAL ORDER NO. 415
PROCEDURE FOR CUSTODY OF WIRE, ORAL OR ELECTRONIC COMMUNICATIONS

Pursuant to Title 18 § 2518(8)(a), the recordings of the contents of any wire, oral, or electronic communication intercepted in accordance with this subsection shall be ordered "sealed" by the Court. Custody of the sealed recordings shall be maintained by the United States Attorney or the Investigative Agency and shall not be destroyed except upon an order of the issuing or denying judge and in any event shall be kept for ten years.

DATED: May 5, 2003   FOR THE COURT:

                                        _____/s/_____

                                         WILLIAM B. SHUBB
                                         Chief Judge
                                         United States Court Judge

F.   *General Order No. 372*

GENERAL ORDER NO. 372
RELATION OF CRIMINAL CASES AND PETITIONER FOR PROBATION ACTION OR VIOLATIONS OF SUPERVISED RELEASE

Good cause appearing, IT IS HEREBY ORDERED as follows:

Where a Notice of Related Cases is filed suggesting that a petition for probation action and/or violation of the terms of supervised release should be related to a new indictment, and the basis of the probation petition or alleged supervised release violation is the conduct underlying the new indictment, the two cases shall be related and the judge assigned to the new criminal case shall also be assigned the earlier case, unless the original sentencing judge desires to retain the first case, in which circumstance both the cases shall be assigned to the original sentencing judge.

This Order supersedes General Order No. 275.

DATED: October 12, 1999

FOR THE COURT:

_____/s/_____
WILLIAM B. SHUBB
Chief Judge
Eastern District of California

This page intentionally left blank.

This page intentionally left blank.

PART II

DISTRICT JUDGES

Hon. Garland E. Burrell, Jr.
District Judge

Chambers Information
U.S. District Court, Eastern District of California
Courtroom No. 10
501 I Street
Sacramento, CA 95814

Scheduling Information
Courtroom Deputy: (916) 930-4114

Biographical Information
Born 1947 in Los Angeles, CA

Federal Judicial Service:
- Judge, U. S. District Court, Eastern District of California
- Nominated by George H.W. Bush on August 1, 1991, to a new seat created by 104 Stat. 5089; Confirmed by the Senate on February 27, 1992, and received commission on March 2, 1992. Served as chief judge, 2007-2008.

Education:
- California State University, Los Angeles, B.A., 1972
- Washington University in St. Louis, M.S.W., 1976
- California Western School of Law, San Diego, J.D., 1976

Professional Career:
- U.S. Marine Corps, 1966-1968
- Deputy District Attorney, Sacramento, California, 1976-1978
- Deputy City Attorney, Sacramento, California, 1978-1979
- Deputy Chief, Civil Division, U.S. Attorney's Office, Eastern District of California, 1979-85
- Business Litigator, Stockman Law Corporation, 1985-1986
- Senior Deputy Attorney, Sacramento, California, 1986-1990
- Chief, Civil Division, U.S. Attorney's Office, Eastern District of California, 1990-1992

Hon. Morrison C. England, Jr.
District Judge

Chambers Information
U.S. District Court, Eastern District of California
Courtroom No. 7
501 I Street
Sacramento, CA 95814

Scheduling Information
Courtroom Deputy: (916) 930-4207

Biographical Information
Born 1954 in St. Louis, MO

Federal Judicial Service:
- Judge, U. S. District Court, Eastern District of California
- Nominated by George W. Bush on March 21, 2002, to a seat vacated by Lawrence K. Karlton; Confirmed by the Senate on August 1, 2002, and received commission on August 2, 2002.

Education:
- University of the Pacific, B.A., 1977
- University of the Pacific, McGeorge School of Law, J.D., 1983

Professional Career:
- U.S. Army Reserve, 1988-present
- Private Practice, California, 1983-1996
- Judge, Sacramento Superior Court for the State of California, 1996-2002

I.   **Judge England's Procedures and Practices**

I.   **CIVIL LAW AND MOTION**
- **Available Hearing Dates (subject to change without notice)**
- Hearing dates are **NOT** reserved. All hearing dates are at 2:00 p.m. in Courtroom 7. Please file your motion(s) in accordance with the Local and Federal Rules of Court. The following are available hearing dates for 2012:
  - January 12, 26
  - February 9, 23
  - March 8, 22
  - April 5, 19
  - May 3, 17, 31
  - June 14, 28
  - July 12, 26
  - August 9, 23
  - September 6, 20
  - October 4, 18
  - November 1, 15, 29
  - December 13
- **Page Limitations**
  - As set forth in the Court's Order Requiring Joint Status Report, any briefs or other papers filed prior to the issuance of the Pretrial (Status) Scheduling Order shall not exceed twenty (20) pages.
  - As set forth in the Court's Pretrial (Status) Scheduling Order, the Court places a page limit on dispositive motions of twenty (20) pages on all initial moving papers, twenty (20) pages on oppositions, and ten (10) pages for replies.
  - Any party wishing to file lengthier documents must first seek relief from said page limitation requirement from the Court.
- **Courtesy Copies**
  - Pursuant to Local rule 133(f), please provide courtesy paper copies of all documents in excess of twenty-five (25) pages or fifty (50) pages for attachments and or exhibits.
  - Delivery of courtesy copies should go directly to the Office of the Clerk (not to chambers) located on the 4th floor.
- **Emailing of Proposed Orders**
  - Pursuant to Local Rule 137(b), regarding the requirements for proper filing of a proposed order, you are required to email the proposed order (in WordPerfect or Microsoft Word) to chambers at: mceorders@caed.uscourts.gov, in addition to filing the pdf version via the CM/ECF system. Pursuant to Local Rule 101, the definition for signature, you may enter /s/ for signatures for all counsel.

- ○ Pursuant to Local Rule 137(b), the email must contain the case number in the subject line.
- **Tentative Rulings**
  - ○ Judge England **DOES NOT** issue tentative rulings.
- **Submitted Motions**
  - ○ Motions submitted by the Court without oral argument are noticed on the docket and public calendar not later than 2 p.m. the day before the hearing date.
  - ○ Please contact the Courtroom Deputy Clerk **after** this time if you have a question regarding a hearing on calendar.
- **Telephonic Appearance**
  - ○ Any party seeking to appear telephonically must file, for the Court's consideration, **not later than seven (7) court days prior to the hearing date**, a Request to Appear Telephonically with a Proposed Order.
  - ○ Upon e-filing the request and proposed order, the proposed order must be emailed to Judge England's email address, in accordance with Local Rule 137(b), for his review and approval at: mceorders@caed.uscourts.gov.
  - ○ The Request MUST contain the DIRECT telephone number for the party(ies) requesting to appear telephonically.
  - ○ If the request is granted, the courtroom deputy clerk will initiate the telephone call 5-10 minutes prior to the time of the scheduled hearing through the court's telephone conferencing system in the courtroom.
  - ○ The Eastern District of California does not utilize the services of Court Call.
- **Discovery Matters (including motions)**
  - ○ Pursuant to Local Rule 302, all discovery matters and other duties shall be noticed before the assigned Magistrate Judge, unless otherwise ordered by the Court.

II. **CRIMINAL LAW AND MOTION**
- **Available Hearing Dates (subject to change without notice)**
- Hearing dates are **NOT** reserved. All hearing dates, including motions, are at 9:00 a.m. in Courtroom 7. Please file your motion(s) in accordance with the Local and Federal Rules of Court. The following are available criminal law and motion calendar dates for 2012:
  - ○ January 5, 12
  - ○ February 2, 9, 16, 23
  - ○ March 1, 8, 15, 22, 29
  - ○ April 5, 12, 26
  - ○ May 3, 10, 17, 24, 31

- ○ June 7, 14, 21, 28
- ○ July 5, 12, 19, 26
- ○ August 2, 23, 30
- ○ September 6, 13, 20, 27
- ○ October 4, 11, 18, 25
- ○ November 1, 8, 15, 29
- ○ December 6, 13

- **Request for Continuance and Proposed Order**
  - ○ The Court would **prefer** the submission of a stipulation and proposed order on any matters that can be handled without an in-court hearing.
  - ○ Stipulations and proposed orders for continuances must be submitted not later than 5 p.m. the Tuesday prior to the hearing date, unless otherwise notified by the Courtroom Deputy Clerk.
  - ○ Pursuant to Local Rule 137(b), regarding the requirements for proper filing of a proposed order, you are required to email the proposed order (in WordPerfect or Microsoft Word) to chambers at: mceorders@caed.uscourts.gov, in addition to filing the pdf version via the CM/ECF system. Pursuant to Local Rule 101, the definition for signature, you may enter /s/ for signatures for all counsel.
  - ○ Pursuant to Local Rule 137(b), the email must contain the case number in the subject line.

- **Telephonic Appearance**
  - ○ Any party seeking to appear telephonically must file, for the Court's consideration, not later than one week prior to the hearing date, a Request to Appear Telephonically with a Proposed Order.
  - ○ Upon e-filing the request and proposed order, the proposed order must be emailed to Judge England's email address, in accordance with Local Rule 137(b), for his review and approval at: mceorders@caed.uscourts.gov.
  - ○ The Request MUST contain the DIRECT telephone number for the party(ies) requesting to appear telephonically.
  - ○ If the request is granted, the courtroom deputy clerk will initiate the telephone call 5-10 minutes prior to the time of the scheduled hearing through the court's telephone conferencing system in the courtroom.
  - ○ The Eastern District of California does not utilize the services of Court Call.

- **Interpreter Services**
  - ○ It is the responsibility of counsel to arrange for the services of an interpreter prior to the scheduled hearing date.
  - ○ It is also the responsibility of counsel to cancel the services of an interpreter prior to the scheduled hearing date.

- ○ Interpreter services for a hearing may be arranged by contacting, Yolanda Riley-Portal, with the Court's Interpreter Office, at 916-930-4221 or YRiley-Portal@caed.uscourts.gov.

III. **TRANSCRIPT ORDERS**
- Transcript orders may be placed with Judge England's court reporter, Diane Shepard, at (916) 554.7460 or DShepard@caed.usourts.gov.

IV. **TRIAL INFORMATION**
- **Days and hours for trial are as follows**
  - ○ Monday 9:00 a.m. - 4:30 p.m.
  - ○ Tuesday 9:00 a.m. - 4:30 p.m.
  - ○ Wednesday 9:00 a.m. - 4:30 p.m.
  - ○ Breaks are at 10:30 a.m., 12:00 p.m. and 3:00 p.m.
  - ○ If Monday is a holiday, the Court will commence trial on Tuesday.
- **Exhibits**
  - ○ The parties are directed to comply with the Court's Final Pretrial Order regarding the preparation and submission of trial exhibits. Questions should be directed to the Courtroom Deputy Clerk.
  - ○ The parties are advised to mark their trial exhibits **exactly as outlined in the Court's Final Pretrial Order**.
  - ○ Exhibit stickers may be obtained from the Office of the Clerk located at 501 I Street, Suite 4-200, Sacramento, California 95814. Questions regarding exhibit stickers should be directed to the Office of the Clerk at 916-930-4000.
- **Lodging of Deposition Transcripts**
  - ○ The parties are directed to comply with the Court's Final Pretrial Order regarding the use of and lodging deposition transcripts for trial. Questions should be directed to the Courtroom Deputy Clerk.

V. **AUDIO VISUAL EQUIPMENT**
The Sacramento Clerk's office has a variety of audio visual equipment available to use for trial purposes. Available equipment may include: ELMOs, projectors, plasma screens, TVs and VCRs. In order to learn about the equipment provided by the court, you can access our intranet home page and follow these procedures:

1) From the Court intranet home page, select Attorney Info tab.

2) Scroll down to Electronic Courtroom option.

3) Attorneys should arrange through the Courtroom Deputy a time to meet with court Information Technology staff for training on electronic equipment. Appointments should be scheduled at least one to two weeks prior to trial.

Hon. Edward J. Garcia

District Judge

Chambers Information

U.S. District Court, Eastern District of California
Courtroom No. 8
501 I Street
Sacramento, CA 95814

Scheduling Information

Courtroom Deputy: (916) 930-4225

Biographical Information

Born 1928

Federal Judicial Service:

- Judge, U. S. District Court, Eastern District of California
- Nominated by Ronald Reagan on February 16, 1984, to a seat vacated by Philip C. Wilkins;
Confirmed by the Senate on March 13, 1984, and received commission on March 14, 1984.
Assumed senior status on November 24, 1996.

Education:

- Sacramento City College, A.A., 1951
- McGeorge School of Law, LL.B., 1958

Professional Career:

- U.S. Army Air Corps, 1946-1949
- Deputy District Attorney, Sacramento County, California, 1959-1964
- Supervising Deputy District Attorney, Sacramento County, California, 1964-1969
- Chief Deputy District Attorney, Sacramento County, California, 1969-1972
- Judge, Sacramento Municipal Court, California, 1972-1984

I.   **Judge Garcia's Procedures and Practices**

    A.   Courtesy Copies of All Motion-Related Pleadings 25 pages or more ONLY: Shall be mailed in hard copy form directly to Judge Garcia's chambers (at the address listed above) immediately upon e-filing pursuant to Local Rules 130(b), 133(f), 133(j).

    B.   E-Mailing of Proposed Orders: As required by the Local Rule 137(b), counsel shall submit their proposed order accompanying any application, request, stipulation or motion in either **Word Perfect (preferred)** or **Microsoft Word** format via email to EJGorders@caed.uscourts.gov. Pursuant to Local Rule 101, the document should include the attorneys' electronic signature(s) (*i.e.*, **/s/ First/Last name**), as well as the date the document was signed.

    C.   CRIMINAL CALENDAR: Held on Mondays at 10:00 a.m. on Fridays. Please contact the courtroom deputy for a new hearing date prior to seeking the continuance of any matters. When applicable, the probation officers shall be included in discussions about continuances. **NO MATTERS ARE CONTINUED WITHOUT THE JUDGE'S PRIOR CONSENT.** If you cannot confirm via telephone, email or ECF about a continuance, check the "drop" portion on the web calendar.

    D.   TRANSCRIPT ORDERS: If you wish to order a transcript please contact the courtroom deputy.

    E.   TRIALS

Trial hours: Jury Selection/Start of Trial Mondays at 8:30 am.

For any paraphernalia (i.e., large physical items or blowups, electronic equipment, etc.): Counsel are to make arrangements through the Court Security Officers at (916) 930-2080.

Counsel rooms are available on either side of the courtroom (out in the hallway) for your use during trial.

Counsel shall lodge any certified transcripts with the courtroom deputy on the first day of trial.

Counsel should also email the courtroom deputy a copy of their exhibit and witness lists in either Word Perfect (preferred) or Microsoft Word format prior to the day of trial (preferably by the Friday prior to trial.) to the following email address: clydon@caed.uscourts.gov.

If you have not already done so, please be sure to email the Word Perfect (preferred) or Microsoft Word version of your proposed jury instructions, voir dire questions and proposed verdict form, or proposed findings of fact (if your case is a bench trial), to the judge's email address: EJGorders@caed.uscourts.gov as required.

F.   **AUDIO/VISUAL EQUIPMENT:** The Sacramento Clerk's office has a variety of audio/visual equipment available to use for trial purposes. Available equipment may include: ELMOs, projectors, plasma screens, Internet hookups, TVs and VCRs. In order to learn about the equipment provided by the court, you can access our intranet home page and follow these procedures:

1) From the Court intranet home page, select Attorney Info tab.\

2) Scroll down to Electronic Courtroom option.

3) Attorneys should arrange a time to meet with court Information Technology staff for reservation of and training on electronic equipment. The Courtroom Deputy can provide contact information with IT. Appointments for training should include all trial counsel and should be scheduled no later than 7 days prior to trial. The court requires the trial counsel to be fully trained and responsible for the operation of any of the technical equipment.

If you have any questions or need further information, please contact the Contact Courtroom Deputy, Colleen Lydon, **(916) 930-4225**.

Hon. Anthony W. Ishii
Chief District Judge

Chambers Information

U.S. District Court, Eastern District of California
Courtroom No. 2
2500 Tulare Street
Fresno, CA 93721

Scheduling Information

Courtroom Deputy: (559) 499-5668

Civil Law and Motion	Mondays at 1:30 p.m.
Criminal Cases	Mondays at 9:00 a.m.
Trials	Tuesdays at 8:30 a.m.

Biographical Information

Born 1946 in Santa Ana, CA

Federal Judicial Service:

- Judge, U. S. District Court, Eastern District of California
- Nominated by William J. Clinton on February 12, 1997, to a seat vacated by Robert E. Coyle; Confirmed by the Senate on October 9, 1997, and received commission on October 14, 1997. Served as chief judge, 2008-present.

Education:

- Reedley Junior College, A.S., 1966
- University of the Pacific School of Pharmacy, Ph.G., 1970
- University of California, Berkeley, Boalt Hall School of Law, J.D., 1973

Professional Career:

- Deputy City Attorney, City Attorney's Office, Sacramento, California, 1975
- Deputy Public Defender, Public Defender's Office, County of Fresno, CA, 1979
- Private Practice, Fresno, California, 1979-1983
- Justice Court Judge, Parlier-Selma Judicial District, County of Fresno, CA, 1983-1993
- Municipal Court Judge, Central Valley Municipal Court, County of Fresno, CA, 1994-1997

I. **Judge Ishii's Procedures and Practices**

1.   Civil law and motion calendar is heard on Mondays only at 1:30 p.m. in Courtroom #2, Eighth floor. It is not necessary to clear a date prior to scheduling law and motion. The parties are required to comply with Local Rule 230, or other applicable rules and notice requirements.

2.   If combined supporting papers or opposition papers exceed 25 pages, the parties are required to submit a complete set of all papers as a chambers courtesy copy, properly tabbed and fastened.

3.   The Court requires Joint Pretrial statements. The statements must be filed seven days before the hearing date and e-mailed as a WordPerfect 8.0 or Word document to: awiorders@caed.uscourts.gov.

4.   All Criminal Cases will be heard on Mondays at 9:00 a.m. unless prior approval for a different time is given by the court. Any changes to the Monday law and motion calendar **MUST** be approved by the court no later than 12:00 Noon on the Thursday prior to the hearing.

5.   All Criminal and Civil trials will begin on Tuesdays at 8:30am.

6.   If you have any additional questions please contact Harold Nazaroff, Courtroom Deputy Clerk, by e-mail at hnazaroff@caed.uscourts.gov

Hon. Lawrence K. Karlton
District Judge

Chambers Information
U.S. District Court, Eastern District of California
Courtroom No. 4
501 I Street
Sacramento, CA 95814

Scheduling Information
Courtroom Deputy: (916) 930-4133

Biographical Information
Born 1935 in Brooklyn, NY

Federal Judicial Service:
- Judge, U. S. District Court, Eastern District of California
- Nominated by Jimmy Carter on June 5, 1979, to a seat vacated by Thomas J. MacBride; Confirmed by the Senate on July 23, 1979, and received commission on July 24, 1979. Served as chief judge, 1983-1990. Assumed senior status on May 28, 2000.

Education:
- Columbia Law School, J.D., 1958

Professional Career:
- U.S. Army, 1958-1960
- Civilian Legal Officer, Sacramento Army Depot, 1960-1962
- Private Practice, Sacramento, California, 1962-1976
- Judge, Superior Court of California, Sacramento County, 1976-1979

I. **Judge Karlton's Procedures and Practices**

CIVIL LAW AND MOTION:
Available dates are: **February 27th, March 12th, March 26th, April 9th and April 23rd all at 10:00 a.m.**, in Courtroom No. 4. You do not need to reserve these dates. [Judge Karlton does not issue tentative rulings.]

Courtesy Copies of all Motion Pleadings:
Shall be submitted in hard copy form immediately upon e-filing pursuant to Local Rule 7-130(b), 5-133(f), 5-133(j).

E-Mailing of Pleadings:
At the time of filing a motion, opposition, or reply, counsel are directed to email a copy in word processing format to lkk-pleadings@caed.uscourts.gov.

E-Mailing of Proposed Orders:
As required by the rules, counsel shall submit via email to lkkorders@caed.uscourts.gov the proposed order accompanying any application, request, stipulation or motion in either Word Perfect (preferred) or Miscrosoft Word format. Pursuant to Local Rule 1-101, the document should include the attorney's electronic signature(s) (i.e., /s/ First/Last name), as well as the date the document was signed.

Page Limitations:
Unless prior permission has been granted, memorandum of law and support of and in opposition to motions are limited to thirty (30) pages, and reply memorandum are limited to fifteen (15) pages. The parties are also cautioned against filing multiple briefs to circumvent this rule.

Hon. John A. Mendez
District Judge

Chambers Information
U.S. District Court, Eastern District of California
Courtroom No. 6
501 I Street
Sacramento, CA 95814

Scheduling Information
Courtroom Deputy: (916) 930-4091

Biographical Information
Born 1955 in Oakland, CA

Federal Judicial Service:
- Judge, U. S. District Court, Eastern District of California
- Nominated by George W. Bush on September 6, 2007, to a seat vacated by David F. Levi; Confirmed by the Senate on April 10, 2008, and received commission on April 17, 2008.

Education:
- Stanford University, B.A., 1977
- Harvard Law School, J.D., 1980

Professional Career:
- Private Practice, California, 1980-1984, 1986-1992, 1993-2001
- Assistant U.S. Attorney, U.S. Attorney's Office, Northern District of California, 1984-1986
- U.S. Attorney for the Northern District of California, 1992-1993
- Judge, Sacramento County Superior Court, California, 2001-2008

Hon. Kimberly J. Mueller
District Judge

Chambers Information
U.S. District Court, Eastern District of California
Courtroom No. 3
501 I Street
Sacramento, CA 95814

Scheduling Information
Courtroom Deputy: (916) 930-4193

Civil Law and Motion	Fridays at 10:00 a.m.
Criminal Law and Motion	Wednesdays at 9:00 a.m.

Biographical Information
Born 1957 in Newton, Kansas

Federal Judicial Service:
- Judge, U. S. District Court, Eastern District of California
- Nominated by Barack Obama on March 10, 2010, to a seat vacated by Frank C. Damrell, Jr.;
Confirmed by the Senate on December 16, 2010, and received commission on December 21, 2010.
-U.S. Magistrate Judge, U.S. District Court, Eastern District of California, 2003-2010

Education:
- Pomona College, B.A., 1981
- Stanford Law School, J.D., 1995

Professional Career:
- Private practice, Sacramento, California, 1995-1999
- Adjunct professor, University of California Davis School of Law, Davis, California, 1999
- Private practice, Sacramento, California, 2000-2003
- Adjunct professor, University of the Pacific, Sacramento, California, 2000-2001

I.   **Judge Mueller's Procedures and Practices**

CIVIL LAW AND MOTION

Civil law and motion calendar is held on designated Fridays at 10:00 a.m., in Courtroom 3, 15th Floor. The next available motion dates are: **March 23, April 20 and 27, May 18, June 8 and 22, 2012.**

JUDGE MUELLER DOES NOT ISSUE TENTATIVE RULINGS.

MOTION DATES ARE SUBJECT TO CHANGE WITHOUT NOTICE.

MOTION DATES ARE NOT RESERVED. File your papers in accordance with the Local and Federal Rules. As set forth in the court's Order Requiring Joint Status Report, any briefs or other papers filed prior to the issuance of the Pretrial (Status) Scheduling Order, the court's standing orders and case specific orders shall not exceed twenty (20) pages. The court also places a page limit for dispositive motions of twenty (20) pages on all initial moving papers, twenty (20) pages on oppositions, and ten (10) pages for replies. The parties are not to file multiple or supplemental briefs to circumvent this rule.

- **Courtesy Copies of All Motion-Related Pleadings and Exhibits totaling 25 pages or more ONLY:** Shall be mailed in hard copy form directly to Judge Mueller's chambers (at the address listed above) immediately upon e-filing as provided by Local Rules 130(b), 133(f) and 133(j).

- **Pagination of Exhibits:** Multi-page exhibits shall be internally paginated, with the pagination for each exhibit beginning with the number one; reference to those exhibits shall refer to the exhibit designation and page number, i.e., Ex. A at 7; Ex. B at 1, etc.

- **E-Mailing of Proposed Orders:** As required by the Local Rule 137(b), counsel shall submit their proposed order accompanying any application, request, stipulation or motion in either Word Perfect (strongly preferred) or Microsoft Word format via email to: kjmorders@caed.uscourts.gov. As provided by Local Rule 101 and 131 (c) and (e), the document should include the attorneys' electronic signature(s) (i.e., /s/ First/Last name), as well as the date the document was signed.

- **Discovery matters (including motions):** All discovery matters and other duties to be performed by the Magistrate Judge pursuant to Local Rule 302 shall be noticed before the assigned Magistrate Judge, unless otherwise ordered by the court.

- **Ex Parte Applications:** Ex Parte Applications are not heard, but are submitted by the court unless otherwise notified. The filer is required to contact the courtroom deputy and the opposing party prior to the filing of the ex parte application in order to advise that such request is being made. The filer shall include an affidavit indicating a satisfactory explanation for the following: 1) the need for the issuance of such an order; 2) the failure of the filer to obtain such a stipulation for the issuance of such an order from other counsel or parties in the action, and 3) why such request cannot be noticed on the court's law and motion calendar pursuant to Local Rule 230. In addition, the document(s) must indicate whether or not an opposition will be filed. Any opposition shall be filed no later than 48 hours from the filing of the ex parte application. When an ex parte application is filed on a Friday, the time for filing the opposition is extended to 72 hours from the filing.

- **Requests for Telephonic Appearances (in civil cases):** Unless the court has ordered personal appearance (for example, as it does with respect to initial scheduling conferences) parties may request telephonic appearance. Any request for appearance by telephone must be prepared in pleading form, along with a proposed order and e-filed accordingly at least 5 days prior to the hearing date. The request and proposed order MUST include the following: 1) the reasons for such request; 2) the name of the attorney(s) making the appearance; and 3) the direct telephone number where the attorney(s) can be reached on the day of the hearing. Upon e-filing the request, a Word Perfect (strongly preferred) or Microsoft Word version of the proposed order must be submitted to the judge's email address for her review and approval: kjmorders@caed.uscourts.gov. If the request is approved, the courtroom deputy will provide conference call information to the attorney. The attorney shall call into the conference line 5 -10 minutes prior to the time of the hearing and be prepared to proceed when his or her matter is called. If counsel encounters problems when accessing the conference line, they should immediately email the Courtroom Deputy at cschultz@caed.uscourts.gov.

CRIMINAL CALENDAR

Beginning in 2012, criminal law and motion calendar will be held on Mondays at 8:30 a.m., unless Monday is a holiday then the criminal calendar will be held on Tuesday at 8:30 a.m. Please contact the courtroom deputy for a new hearing date prior to seeking the continuance of any sentencing matters.

NO MATTERS ARE CONTINUED WITHOUT THE JUDGE'S PRIOR CONSENT.

THE COURT REQUIRES PERSONAL APPEARANCES EVERY THREE MONTHS FOR STATUS CONFERENCES UNLESS GOOD CAUSE AND ALL APPLICABLE LAWS SUPPORT LONGER INTERVALS AND THE COURT APPROVES A WRITTEN REQUEST IN ADVANCE.

- **Criminal Calendar Continuances:** The court requires the submission of stipulations and proposed orders on any matters that can be handled without an in-court hearing (e.g., request for the setting of further status conferences, requests for continuances of pending matters, or the setting of trial confirmation hearings and trial dates). Any such stipulation shall include the date of the last appearance by the parties, explain in detail the reason for a requested continuance and include all language required by law. When applicable, the probation officers shall be included in discussions about continuances. Stipulations and requests for continuances on criminal matters shall be submitted no later than noon on the Thursday prior to the hearing date, unless the Courtroom Deputy notifies counsel otherwise. If you cannot confirm a continuance via telephone, email or ECF, check the "off-calendar" portion on the web calendar.

- **Motions and Pagination of Exhibits:** The court has placed page limits as follows: twenty (20) pages on all initial moving papers, twenty (20) pages on oppositions, and ten (10) pages for replies. The parties are not to file multiple or supplemental briefs to circumvent this rule. Multi-page exhibits shall be internally paginated, with the pagination for each exhibit beginning with the number one; reference to those exhibits shall refer to the exhibit designation and page number, i.e., Ex. A at 7; Ex. B at 1, etc.

- **Requests for Telephonic Appearances (in criminal cases):** Any request for appearance by telephone must be prepared in pleading form, along with a proposed order and e-filed accordingly at least 5 days prior to the hearing date. The request and proposed order MUST include the following: 1) the reasons for such request; 2) the name of the attorney(s) making the appearance; and 3) the direct telephone number where the attorney(s) can be reached on the day of hearing. Upon e-filing the request, a Word Perfect (strongly preferred) or Microsoft Word version of the proposed order must be submitted to the judge's email address for her review and approval: kjmorders@caed.uscourts.gov. If the request is approved, the courtroom deputy will provide conference call information to the attorney. The attorney shall call into the conference line 5 -10 minutes prior to the time of the hearing and be prepared to proceed when his or her matter is called. If counsel encounters problems when accessing the conference line, they should immediately email the Courtroom Deputy at cschultz@caed.uscourts.gov.

- **Rule 17(c) Subpoena Requests:** These requests should be submitted to the duty magistrate judge.

SETTLEMENT CONFERENCES: Held on available Friday mornings unless otherwise ordered by the Court.

TRANSCRIPT ORDERS: If you wish to order a transcript please contact Cathie Bodene at (916) 446-6360 or cbodene@caed.uscourts.gov.

TRIALS

Judge Mueller utilizes a modified Arizona plan for jury selection. The court will conduct voir dire and allow short voir dire by counsel then ascertain if any potential juror will be excused for cause. If a potential juror is excused for cause, a new name is selected and that person is voir dired before jury selection continues. Once voir dire is completed and all challenges for cause have been ruled on, the attorneys will be given a strike sheet to exercise their peremptory challenges. Once the peremptory challenges are marked, the Judge will excuse those jurors and then the highest numbered jurors still in the box until the desired number of jurors remain.

Presumptive trial hours, subject to adjustment based on the other court calendars: Jury Selection/Start of Trial Mondays at 1:30 p.m. - 4:30 p.m., additional days Tuesdays - Thursdays 8:30 a.m. - 1:30 p.m., and dark on Fridays. Lunch on full days is 12:00 p.m. - 1:30 p.m., and breaks on other days are at 10:15 a.m. and 11:45

a.m. If Monday is a holiday, then trial shall commence on Tuesday of that week at 1:30 p.m.

Electronic Equipment: Judge Mueller's courtroom is currently equipped with the following electronic equipment: 1) ELMO (limited availability), 2) Video Cable Hook-ups; 3) Large Projector Screen; 4) Laptop Hook-ups; and 5) Monitors in jury box, witness stand, and at counsel table. The courthouse also has a projector available. However, counsel should contact the courtroom deputy at least 1-2 weeks prior to trial in order to verify the availability of the courthouse projector and ELMO, or counsel may bring in their own, if necessary. Additionally, counsel should contact the courtroom deputy prior to the day of trial in order to make arrangements to view the courtroom and bring in any other necessary equipment and/or materials. Additional equipment is available from the Clerk's office as described below.

For any paraphernalia (e.g., large physical items or blowups, electronic equipment, etc.): Counsel are to make arrangements through the Court Security Officers at (916) 930-2080.

Counsel rooms are available on either side of the courtroom (out in the hallway) for your use during trial.

Counsel shall lodge any certified transcripts with the courtroom deputy on the first day of trial.

Counsel also shall email the courtroom deputy copies of exhibit and witness lists in either Word Perfect (strongly preferred) or Microsoft Word format by the Thursday prior to trial to the following email address: cschultz@caed.uscourts.gov. Exhibit lists shall be in table format and include two columns on the right side of the table, one labeled "offered" and the last labeled "admitted."

Parties are to use the following template for Exhibit List: Exhibit List Template.

Counsel shall comply with the Court's Final Pretrial Order regarding the preparation and submission of trial exhibits. Questions should be directed to the Courtroom Deputy. The parties are advised to mark their trial exhibits exactly as outlined in the Court's Final Pretrial Order. Exhibit stickers may be obtained from the Office of the Clerk located at 501 I Street, Suite 4-200, Sacramento, California 95814. Questions regarding exhibit stickers should be directed to the Office of the Clerk at 916-930-4000.

Parties are to use the following template when submitting Jury Instructions:
- Prisoner Pro Se Civil Jury Instructions (Preliminary)
- Civil Pro Se Jury Instructions (Final)
- Civil Pro Se Jury Instructions (Preliminary)
- Civil Jury Instructions (Final)
- Prisoner Civil Jury Instructions (Preliminary)
- Civil Jury Instructions (Preliminary)
- Criminal Jury Instructions (Final)
- Criminal Jury Instructions (Preliminary)

If you have not already done so, please be sure to email the Word Perfect (preferred) or Microsoft Word version of your statement of the case, jury instructions, voir dire questions and proposed verdict form, or proposed findings of fact (if your case is a bench trial), to the judge's email address: kjmorders@caed.uscourts.gov as required.

AUDIO/VISUAL EQUIPMENT

The Sacramento Clerk's office has a variety of audio/visual equipment available to use for trial purposes. Available equipment may include: ELMOs, projectors, plasma screens, TVs and VCRs. In order to learn about the equipment provided by the court, you can access our intranet home page and follow these procedures:

1) From the Court intranet home page, select Attorney Info tab.

2) On the next screen, select Sacramento.

3) Scroll down to Electronic Courtroom option.

4) Attorneys should arrange through the Courtroom Deputy a time to meet with court Information Technology staff for training on electronic equipment. Appointments should be scheduled at least one to two weeks prior to trial.

If you have any questions or need further information, please contact the Contact Courtroom Deputy, Casey Schultz, at 916-930-4193.

Hon. Lawrence J. O'Neill
District Judge

Chambers Information
U.S. District Court, Eastern District of California
Courtroom No. 4
2500 Tulare Street
Fresno, CA 93721

Scheduling Information
Courtroom Deputy: (559) 499-5682

Civil Law and Motion	Mondays through Fridays at 8:30 a.m.
Criminal Law and Motion	Mondays at 8:30 a.m.
Trials	Tuesdays at 8:30 a.m.

Biographical Information
Born 1952 in Oakland, CA

Federal Judicial Service:
- Judge, U. S. District Court, Eastern District of California
- Nominated by George W. Bush on January 9, 2007, to a seat vacated by Oliver W. Wanger; Confirmed by the Senate on February 1, 2007, and received commission on February 2, 2007.
U.S. Magistrate Judge, U.S District Court for the Eastern District of CA, 1999-2007

Education:
- University of California at Berkeley, B.A., 1973
- Golden Gate University, M.P.A., 1976
- University of California, Hastings College of Law, J.D., 1979

Professional Career:
- Police Officer, City of San Leandro, California, 1973-1976
- Law Clerk, Hon. Robert F. Kane, First Appellate Court, California Court of Appeal, 1979
- Private Practice, Fresno, California, 1979-1990
- Adjunct Professor, San Joaquin College of Law, 1986-1992
- Judge, Fresno County Superior Court, California, 1990-1999

I.   Judge O'Neill's Procedures and Practices

1. Civil law and motion calendar is heard Tuesday through Friday at 8:30 a.m. in Courtroom 4, Seventh floor. It is not necessary to clear a date prior to scheduling law and motion. The parties are required to comply with Local Rule 230, or other applicable rules and notice requirements.

2. Unless prior leave of Court is obtained seven days before the filing date, all moving and opposition briefs or legal memorandum in civil cases shall not exceed 25 pages. Reply briefs filed by moving parties shall not exceed 10 pages. Briefs that exceed the page limitations or are sought to be filed without leave may not be considered. If combined supporting papers or opposition papers exceed 25 pages, the parties are required to submit a complete set of all papers as a chambers courtesy copy, properly tabbed and fastened.

3. The Court requires Joint Pretrial statements. The statements must be filed seven days before the hearing date and e-mailed as a WordPerfect 8.0 or Word document to: ljoorders@caed.uscourts.gov.

4. Telephonic appearances before District Judge Lawrence J. O'Neill are encouraged. The parties may appear at hearings by telephone by arranging a one line conference call and telephoning the Court at (559) 499-5680.

5. All Criminal Cases will be heard on Mondays at 1:00pm effective 11/14/2011.

6. All Criminal and Civil trials will begin on Tuesdays at 8:30am.

7. If you have any additional questions please contact Irma Munoz, Courtroom Deputy Clerk, by e-mail at imunoz@caed.uscourts.gov.

Hon. William B. Shubb
District Judge

Chambers Information
U.S. District Court, Eastern District of California

Courtroom No. 5	Courtroom No. 3
501 I Street	2500 Tulare Street
Sacramento, CA 95814	Fresno, CA 93721

Scheduling Information
Courtroom Deputy: (916) 930-4234 (Sacramento Division)

Civil Law and Motion	Every Other Monday at 2:00 p.m.
Criminal Law and Motion	Mondays at 9:30 a.m.
Trials	Tuesdays through Fridays from 9:00 a.m. to 4:30 p.m.

Biographical Information
Born 1938 in Oakland, CA

Federal Judicial Service:
- Judge, U. S. District Court, Eastern District of California
- Nominated by George H.W. Bush on August 3, 1990, to a seat vacated by Raul A. Ramirez; Confirmed by the Senate on September 28, 1990, and received commission on October 1, 1990. Served as chief judge, 1996-2003. Assumed senior status on November 1, 2004.

Education:
- University of California, Berkeley, A.B., 1960
- University of California, Berkeley, Boalt Hall School of Law, J.D., 1963

Professional Career:
- Law Clerk, Hon. Sherrill Halbert, U.S. Dist. Court, Eastern Dist. of CA, 1963-1965
- Assistant U.S. Attorney, Eastern District of California, 1965-1971
- Chief Assistant U.S. Attorney, Eastern District of California, 1971-1974
- Private Practice, Sacramento, California, 1974-1980
- U.S. Attorney for the Eastern District of California, 1980-1981
- Private Practice, Sacramento, California, 1981-1990

I. Judge Shubb's Procedures and Practices

All parties are required to adhere to the following information noted below for civil and criminal cases assigned to Judge Shubb. If you are seeking information relating to a particular case, Local Rules, filing procedures, juror details, directions to the courthouse, or general information, such information may also be obtained by accessing our internet website address at www.caed.uscourts.gov. Any inquiries related to the status of signed stipulations and orders can be found by accessing the court docket. If your question cannot be answered by any one of these resources, you may contact the Courtroom Deputy at the telephone number or email address listed above.

I. **CIVIL LAW AND MOTION:** (Judge Shubb d<u>oes</u> **not** issue tentative rulings.)

Held **every other** Monday at 2:00 p.m., in Courtroom 5, 14th Floor. If Monday is a holiday, then the motion shall be heard on Tuesday at 2:00 p.m., unless otherwise notified by the Court.

**NOTE: Counsel shall refer to Local Rule 260 and F.R.Civ.P. 56, and shall confer with the courtroom deputy prior to filing any motions for Summary Judgment, Summary Adjudication, Judgment on the Pleadings or Partial Summary Judgment.

The next available motion dates are: **April 9 and 23; May 7 and 21; and June 4 and 18, 2012 at 2:00 p.m.**

MOTION DATES ARE SUBJECT TO CHANGE WITHOUT NOTICE.

MOTION DATES ARE NOT RESERVED. Simply file your papers in accordance with the Local Rule (see L.R. 230) and Federal Rules. When including case citations, please note that Judge Shubb prefers "The Blue Book" format.

Courtesy Copies of All Motion-Related Pleadings 25 pages or more ONLY: Shall be **mailed** in hard copy form directly to Judge Shubb's chambers (at the address listed above) immediately upon e-filing, and pursuant to Local Rule 130(b) and 133(f).

E-Mailing of Proposed Orders: As required by the rules, counsel shall submit **via email** to WBSorders@caed.uscourts.gov the proposed order accompanying any application, request, stipulation or motion in either **Word Perfect (preferred)** or **Microsoft Word** format. Pursuant to Local Rule 131(c), the document should include the attorneys' electronic signature(s) (i.e., **/s/ First/Last name**), as well as the date the document was signed.

Motions to Tax Costs (Bills of Costs): Motions to tax costs are taken under submission by the court upon initial filing; no hearing date is set. All briefs and responses shall be submitted in accordance with the Local and Federal Rules.

Discovery matters (including motions): All discovery matters and other duties to be performed by the Magistrate Judge pursuant to **Local Rule 302** shall be noticed before the assigned Magistrate Judge, unless otherwise ordered by the Court.

Page Limitations: Judge Shubb currently has no set page limitations, other than what is specified in the Court's Local Rules, or found on the Court's website at: www.caed.uscourts.gov, or as noted in the Federal Rules.

Designation and Submission of Deposition Transcripts: Judge Shubb requires that counsel adhere to Local Rule 133(j), and that a hard copy of the entire certified deposition(s) be submitted to chambers as instructed in said rule.

Requests for Telephonic Appearances (in civil cases): ***Any requests for appearances by telephone must be prepared in pleading form, along with a proposed order and e-filed accordingly **NO LATER THAN 1-2 WEEKS PRIOR** to the hearing date. The request and proposed order **must** include the telephone number where the attorney can be reached on the day of the telephonic appearance. Upon e-filng the request, a Word Perfect (preferred) or Microsoft Word version of the proposed order must be submitted to the judge's email address for his review and approval to: WBSorders@caed.uscourts.gov.

If the request is approved, counsel will receive a separate email notification from the courtroom deputy with instructions on how to participate in the telephone conference call through the court's telephone conferencing service. Counsel shall immediately confirm receipt of said email.

> ***PLEASE NOTE:** Scheduling Conferences are **generally taken off calendar and under submission** within the week prior to the scheduled date, and upon the court's receipt of the properly and timely filed Joint Status Report. Therefore, these matters **are not** usually held via telephone conference. Therefore, after the filing of the Joint Status Report, counsel shall contact the courtroom deputy prior to making any requests for telephone conference appearances at scheduling conferences.

Ex Parte Applications (in civil cases): Ex Parte Applications are **not heard**, but are submitted by the court unless otherwise notified. The filer is **required** to contact the courtroom deputy and the opposing party **prior** to the filing of the ex parte application in order to advise that such request is being made. In addition, the document(s) **must** indicate whether or not an opposition will be filed. The filer shall include an affidavit indicating a satisfactory explanation for the following: 1) the need for the issuance of such an order; 2) the failure of the filer to obtain a stipulation for the issuance of such an order from other counsel or parties in the action, and 3) why such request cannot be noticed on the court's motion calendar pursuant to Local Rule 230.

II. CRIMINAL CALENDAR INFORMATION

Held on Mondays at _9:30 a.m._ in Courtroom 5, 14th Floor; unless Monday is a holiday, then set for Tuesday at 9:30 a.m. Please contact the courtroom deputy for a new hearing date prior to seeking the continuance of any criminal matters.

NOTE: Any hearing dates to be scheduled for an upcoming Monday criminal calendar during Criminal Duty on a Friday afternoon shall not be set unless first cleared by Judge Shubb's CRD. It is counsel's responsibility to contact this CRD before 12:00 PM (Noon) on that Friday if they know, or if there is any possibility, that they wish to have a defendant placed on the upcoming Monday criminal calendar. Otherwise, the next available criminal calendar hearing date is to be set.

In addition, any requests made by counsel for the setting of TCH and Trial dates during the criminal duty calendar must first be cleared through this CRD. Therefore, counsel MUST contact this CRD prior to the criminal duty calendar if they know, or if there is any possibility, that they wish to have said dates set.

Criminal Calendar Continuances: Please note that the Court would **prefer** the submission of stipulations and proposed orders on any matters that can be handled without an in-court hearing (i.e., request for the setting of further status conferences, requests for continuances of pending matters, or the setting of trial confirmation hearings and trial dates). Please contact the Courtroom Deputy for available hearing dates prior to submitting your stipulations. **Stipulations and Requests for continuances on criminal matters, other than sentencings, shall be submitted no later than 12:00 (Noon) on the Friday prior to the hearing date, unless otherwise notified by the Courtroom Deputy. Stipulations and Requests for continuances of sentencings shall be submitted no later than 12:00 (Noon) on the Thursday prior to the hearing date, unless otherwise notified by the Courtroom Deputy.**

Criminal Motions and Procedures: Counsel shall refer to **Local Rule 430.1** for the filing of criminal motions. Criminal motions calendared before Judge Shubb shall be heard on a Monday at 9:30 a.m. If Monday is a holiday, then the motion shall be set for Tuesday at 9:30 a.m., unless otherwise ordered by the Court.

**MOTION DATES ARE NOT RESERVED. Simply file your papers in accordance with the Local Rule (see L.R. 430.1) and Federal Rules. When including case citations, please note that Judge Shubb prefers "The Blue Book" format.

Interpreter Services: It is the responsibility of counsel to arrange for the services of an interpreter prior to the scheduled hearing date. It is also the responsibility of counsel to cancel the services of an interpreter prior to the scheduled hearing date. Interpreter services for a hearing may be arranged by contacting, Yolanda Riley-Portal, with the Court's Interpreter Office, at 916-

930-4221 or YRiley-Portal@caed.uscourts.gov.

III. **TRANSCRIPT ORDERS**

Please contact the Court Reporter **directly** for any transcript requests: Kathy Swinhart at (916) 446-1347 or via email at kswinhartcsr@gmail.com. If you wish to order a transcript for a hearing that occurred **prior to August 13, 2007**, please contact Kelly O'Halloran at (916) 448-2712

IV. **TRIAL INFORMATION**

Trial hours: Normally 9:00 am - 4:30 pm – Tues. - Fri.; Lunch Time 1 - 1 1/2hours (usually 12 - 1:30 pm), <u>unless otherwise notified by the Court</u>. If Monday is a holiday, then trial shall commence on Wednesday of that week.

Electronic Equipment: Judge Shubb's courtroom is currently equipped with the following electronic equipment: 1) ELMO (limited availability), 2) Video Cable Hook-ups; 3) Large Projector Screen; 4) Laptop Hook-ups; 5) Monitors in jury box, witness stand, and at counsel table; 6) Wireless Microphones; and 7) Lapel Microphones. The courthouse also has a projector available. However, counsel should contact the courtroom deputy at least 1-2 weeks prior to trial in order to verify the availability of the courthouse projector and ELMO, or counsel may bring in their own, if necessary. Additionally, counsel should contact the courtroom deputy prior to the day of trial in order to make arrangements to view the courtroom and bring in any other necessary equipment and/or materials.

For any paraphernalia (i.e., large physical items or blowups, electronic equipment, etc.): Counsel are to make arrangements through the Court Security Officers at (916) 930-2080, **if necessary**.

Counsel rooms are available on either side of the courtroom (out in the hallway) for your use during trial.

Please make sure to bring two sets of exhibits (1 original set for the witness with exhibit tags (gold for Government, pink for Plaintiff and blue for Defendant(s); and 1 set for the judge). Exhibits should be in **easy-to-use binders (not larger than 3" in width)**, with divider tabs down the side marking each exhibit. Government/Plaintiffs shall mark their exhibits using numbers; Defendants shall mark their exhibits using letters (i.e., A-Z, AA-ZZ, etc.); or, the parties may agree to use certain blocks of numbers, (i.e., 1-100 for plaintiffs, 101-200 for defendants), as long as the parties do not use the same numbers. Otherwise, exhibits shall be marked as ordered in the Pretrial Scheduling order issued by this Court in civil cases. Exhibit tags should be placed on the witness' set of exhibits only. The Court's set <u>does not</u> require exhibit tags, but must include the divider tabs down the side marking each exhibit. Exhibit tags can be obtained through the clerk's office (gold for Government, pink for Plaintiff, blue for Defendant(s)).

Civil Cases: Counsel shall lodge any certified transcripts with the courtroom deputy on the <u>first</u> day of trial.

Counsel should also email the courtroom deputy a copy of their exhibit and witness lists in either Word Perfect (preferred) or Microsoft Word format, no **later than the Friday prior to scheduled trial date**, to the following email address (*see sample of required exhibit list format below*): kkirkseysmith@caed.uscourts.gov.

EXH	DESCRIPTION	IDENTIFIED	ADMITTED
1			
2			
3			

If you have not already done so, please be sure to email the Word Perfect (preferred) or Microsoft Word version of your jury instructions, voir dire questions and proposed verdict form, or proposed findings of fact (if your case is a civil bench trial), to the judge's email address: WBSorders@caed.uscourts.gov as required.

V. **AUDIO/VISUAL EQUIPMENT**

The Sacramento Clerk's office has a variety of audio/visual equipment available to use for trial purposes. Available equipment may include: ELMOs, projectors, plasma screens, TVs and VCRs. In order to learn about the equipment provided by the court, you can access our intranet home page and follow these procedures:

1) From the Court intranet home page, select Attorney Info tab.

2) Scroll down to Electronic Courtroom option.

3) **Attorneys should arrange through the Courtroom Deputy a time to meet with court Information Technology staff for training on electronic equipment. Appointments should be scheduled at least one to two weeks prior to trial.**

If you have any questions or need further information, please contact the Courtroom Deputy, Karen Kirksey Smith, at 916-930-4234.

Hon. Oliver W. Wanger
District Judge

Chambers Information
U.S. District Court, Eastern District of California
Courtroom No. 3
2500 Tulare Street
Fresno, CA 93721

Scheduling Information
Courtroom Deputy: (559) 499-5652

Civil Law and Motion	Mondays at 10:00 a.m. (Court will hear only six civil motions every Monday.)

Biographical Information
Born 1940 in Los Angeles, CA

Federal Judicial Service:
- Judge, U. S. District Court, Eastern District of California
- Nominated by George H.W. Bush on January 8, 1991, to a seat vacated by Milton Lewis Schwartz; Confirmed by the Senate on March 21, 1991, and received commission on March 25, 1991. Assumed senior status on May 31, 2006.

Education:
- University of Southern California, B.S., 1963
- University of California, Berkeley, Boalt Hall School of Law, LL.B., 1966

Professional Career:
- U.S. Marine Corps Reserve Sergeant, 1960-1967
- Deputy District Attorney, Fresno County, 1967-1969
- Adjunct Professor, Humphrey College of Law, 1968-1969
- Private Practice, Fresno, California, 1969-1991
- Adjunct Professor, San Joaquin College of Law, Fresno, California, 1970-1991
- Dean of the Law School, 1980-1983
- City Attorney, City of Mendota, California, 1975-1980
- Temporary Judge, Superior Court of California, County of Fresno, 1988
- *Pro tem* Settlement Conference Judge, Superior Court of CA, County of Fresno, 1989

I.   Judge Wanger's Procedures and Practices

MOTION HEARING DATES: Judge Wanger will hear 6 civil motions every Monday, excluding holidays, at 10:00 a.m.

The next available civil motions date is 9/26/2011 and beyond.

Judge Wanger does not reserve hearing dates. Please file your motion as quickly as possible to ensure your motion will be heard on the next available date. Once 6 motions have been filed on a given hearing date, the Court will continue any motion filed thereafter to the next available hearing date.

Judge Wanger does not provide tentative rulings for civil motions prior to the hearing date.

Any changes to Monday Criminal Calendars must be requested with a stipulation and proposed order or memorandum by 12:00 PM the Thursday before.

TELEPHONIC APPEARANCES: If you are more than 50 miles away from the courthouse you may appear telephonically.

Please contact opposing counsel to see if they also wish to appear telephonically.

You must then coordinate a conference call through an operator or on your internal phone system.

After all parties are on the line, call Judge Wanger's chambers at (559) 499-5650 at the time of the hearing.

If opposing counsel wishes to appear in person, you may still appear telephonically by calling into chambers directly.

Once you have done the above, please contact Courtroom Deputy Renee Gaumnitz at RGaumnitz@caed.uscourts.gov to advise the Court who will be appearing telephonically. Also provide a contact number of the party who is initiating the conference call.

You may contact Courtroom Deputy Renee Gaumnitz for questions regarding any of the above information at RGaumnitz@caed.uscourts.gov.

This page intentionally left blank.

This page intentionally left blank.

MAGISTRATE JUDGES

Hon. Gary S. Austin
Magistrate Judge

Chambers Information
U.S. District Court, Eastern District of California
Courtroom No. 10, 6th Floor
2500 Tulare Street
Fresno, CA 93721

Scheduling Information
Courtroom Deputy: (559) 499-5962

Civil Law and Motion	Fridays at 9:30 a.m.
Settlement Conferences	Mondays through Thursdays at 10:30 a.m.

Biographical Information
Federal Judicial Service:
- U. S. District Court, Eastern District of California
- Appointed as United States Magistrate Judge, October 12, 2007.

Education:
- California State University, Fresno, B.A. Speech Communication, 1972
- San Joaquin College of Law, J.D., 1976

Professional Career:
- Law Clerk/Crier for U.S. District Court Judge M.D. Crocker, Eastern District of California, Fresno, 1976-1977
- Staff Attorney, U.S. Federal Defenders Office, Eastern District of CA, Fresno, 1977
- Fresno County Deputy District Attorney, 1977-1984
- Fresno County Senior Deputy District Attorney and Lead Attorney for the Career Criminal Unit, 1984-1986
- Municipal Court Judge, Consolidated Fresno Judicial District, 1986-1988
- Superior Court Judge, Fresno County Superior Court, 1988-2007

I.   ## Judge Austin's Procedures and Practices

CIVIL LAW & MOTION:

Magistrate Judge Austin hears his civil law and motion calendar on Fridays at 9:30 a.m. Dates DO NOT need to be cleared with the Court. Please pick a Friday that allows time for appropriate processing of the motion, pursuant to Local Rule, and schedule the hearing when filing the motion. If the date conflicts with the Court's calendar, the Court will reschedule the hearing by minute order.

SETTLEMENT CONFERENCES:

Magistrate Judge Austin hears settlement conferences Mondays to Thursdays at 10:30 a.m. These dates DO need to be cleared with the Court.

Hon. Dennis L. Beck
Magistrate Judge

Chambers Information
U.S. District Court, Eastern District of California
Courtroom No. 9, 6th Floor
2500 Tulare Street
Fresno, CA 93721

Scheduling Information
Courtroom Deputy: (559) 499-5672

Civil Law and Motion	Fridays at 9:00 a.m.

Biographical Information
Federal Judicial Service:
- U. S. District Court, Eastern District of California
- Appointed as United States Magistrate Judge, March 12, 1990.
- Chief Magistrate Judge, January 2, 2002-Present

Education:
- College of William and Mary, B.A., 1969
- College of William & Mary, Marshal Wythe School of Law, J.D., 1972

Professional Career:
- Deputy District Attorney, Fresno County, CA, 1972-1977 & 1979
- Chief Deputy District Attorney, Fresno County, CA, 1980-1982
- Superior Court Judge, Kings County, CA, 1983-1985
- Private Practice, Fresno, California, 1978-1979 & 1985-1987
- Assistant District Attorney, Fresno County, CA, 1987-1990

I.   Judge Beck's Procedures and Practices

1.   _Civil Law & Motion Calendar - Judge Beck does NOT issue tentative rulings:_

a) Held on Fridays at 9:00 a.m. in Courtroom #9 - motion dates are not reserved.

b) Parties do not need to clear a motion hearing date. File your moving papers in accordance with the Local and Federal Rules, if the date conflicts with the Court's calendar, the Court will reschedule the matter by minute order. DATES ARE NOT RESERVED.

c) Courtesy Copies of ALL Motion-Related Pleadings: **properly tabbed, fastened, and clearly identified as a "Courtesy Copy" (to avoid duplicate and erroneous filing by court staff)** - shall be mailed in hard copy to the Court, Attn: Judge Beck.

d) on short notice - Minute Orders can be issued vacating the hearing and taking the matter under submission pursuant to Local Rule 230(h) (Fed. R. Civ. P. 78) - please refer to your electronic NEF.
e) Motion dates are subject to change without notice.

2.   _Settlement Conferences:_

a) Parties must appear with counsel.

b) Telephonic appearance: for some parties may be granted BUT a written request with cause must be sent to Judge Beck for approval.

c) Confidential Settlement Conference Statement is MANDATORY from each party, and must be submitted to Judge Beck chambers, at least seven (7) calendar days prior to the Settlement Conference.

3.   _Telephonic Appearance:_

a) Please contact the courtroom deputy if one or more attorneys will be appearing telephonically, so that a notation can be made on the Court's calendar.

b) Plaintiff(s)/defendant(s) counsel shall make arrangements for a conference call with the AT&T operator (if counsel does not have conference call capabilities on their telephone systems), and shall initiate the call at the above-designated time. After all parties are on the line, the call should then be placed to Judge Beck's chambers at (559)499-5670.

Telephonic appearance for out-of-town counsel is greatly encouraged by chambers.

4.   _Scheduling Conference:_

A JOINT Scheduling Conference Report carefully prepared and executed by all counsel, shall be electronically filed in CM/ECF, in full compliance with the requirements set forth in, ORDER SETTING MANDATORY SCHEDULING CONFERENCE Exhibit "A," one (1) full week prior to the Scheduling Conference, and shall be e-mailed, in WordPerfect or Word format, to dlborders@caed.uscourts.gov.

5. **_Telephonic Conference calls re Discovery Disputes:_**

a) Please contact the courtroom deputy, who will give you dates & times for said conference possibilities. Thus contact opposing counsel, select one of those dates & times, then call the courtroom deputy back as to which date the parties preferred.

b) A letter brief must be emailed to the Courtroom Deputy by each counsel, in regards to the Conference Call.

6. **_Discovery hearings:_**

a) Local Rule 251(a) (Fed.R.Civi.P. 37) requires a joint statement: HOWEVER, with the press of business, Judge Beck REQUIRES a joint statement re discovery disagreement be filed seven (7) days before the scheduled hearing date (i.e., the Friday before the customary Friday hearing).

7. **_All documents that require Court Approval:_**

a) As required by the rules, counsel shall submit via email to dlborders@caed.uscourts.gov the proposed order, application, request, stipulation, etc., in either Word Perfect (preferred) or Miscrosoft Word format. Pursuant to Local Rule 131, the document should include the attorney(s) electronic signature(s) (i.e., /s/First/Last name), as well as the date the document was signed.

Hon. Edmund F. Brennan
Magistrate Judge

Chambers Information
U.S. District Court, Eastern District of California
Courtroom No. 24, 8th Floor
501 I Street
Sacramento, CA 95814

Scheduling Information
Courtroom Deputy: (916) 930-4172

Biographical Information
Federal Judicial Service:
- U. S. District Court, Eastern District of California
- Appointed as United States Magistrate Judge, August 21, 2006.

Education:
- Doane College, Cete, NE 1971-1973,
- Southwestern University School of Law Los Angeles, CA 1974-1979, J.D

Professional Career:
- Social Security Administration, 1977-1984
- Law Clerk for U.S. District Judge Edward J. Garcia, Eastern District of California, 1984-1988
- U.S. Attorney's Office, Assistant U.S. Attorney, 1988-1994
- U.S. Attorney's Office, Deputy Chief, Civil Division, 1994-1997
- U.S. Attorney's Office, Chief, Civil Defensive Litigation, 1997-2005
- U.S. Attorney's Office, Chief, Civil Division, 2005-Aug. 21, 2006

Hon. Carolyn K. Delaney
Magistrate Judge

Chambers Information
U.S. District Court, Eastern District of California
Courtroom No. 26, 8th Floor
501 I Street
Sacramento, CA 95814

Scheduling Information
Courtroom Deputy: (916) 930-4004

Biographical Information
Federal Judicial Service:
- U.S District Court, Eastern District of California
- United States Magistrate Judge, appointed August, 2011

Education:
- Wesleyan University, B.A., 1984
- Stanford University, J.D., 1988

Professional Career:
- San Mateo County District Attorney's Office, Redwood City, CA, 1989-1990
- Bucks County District Attorney's Office, Doylestown, PA, 1991-1996
- Pennsylvania Office of Attorney General, Allentown, PA, 1996-1997
- U.S. Attorney's Office, Eastern District of California, 1998-2008
- U.S. Department of Justice, U.S. Embassy, Ankara, Turkey, 2008-2009
- U.S. Attorney's Office, Eastern District of California, 2009-2011

I. **Judge Delaney's Procedures and Practices**

CRIMINAL LAW AND MOTION: Criminal law and motion is heard every Thursday at 9:00 a.m. except when Judge Delaney is "Duty," then her criminal law and motion calendar is held on any "Duty" Calendar at 2:00 PM.

2011 Duty Schedule: August 15-19; October 10-21; and December 19-30.

2011 Petty Offense Schedule: None scheduled.

CIVIL LAW AND MOTION: Civil law and motion is heard every Wednesday at 10:00 a.m. MOTION DATES ARE NOT RESERVED. Simply file your moving papers in accordance with the Local and Federal Rules.

The following dates are available for hearings:
2011:
-November 23, and 30
-December 7, and 14

2012:
-January 4, 11, 18, and 25
-February 1, 8, 15, 22, and 29
-March 7, 14, 21, and 28
-April 4, 11, 18, and 25
-May 2, 9, 16, 23, and 30
-June 6, 13, 20, and 27

Telephonic Appearance: Parties interested in appearing by telephone must file a request and proposed order.

Proposed Orders: As required by the local rules, counsel shall submit via email, to ckdorders@caed.uscourts.gov, the proposed order accompanying any application, request, stipulation or motion in either Word Perfect or Microsoft Word format. Pursuant to Local Rule 131 (c), the document should include the attorneys' electronic signature(s) (i.e., /s/ First/Last name), as well as the date the document was signed.

TRANSCRIPT ORDERS: If you wish to order a transcript for a hearing held before Magistrate Judge Carolyn K. Delaney (or another Magistrate Judge in the Eastern District-Sacramento Division), you will need to complete the *Electronic Court Reporter Transcript Order Form or the Appeal Transcript Designation and Order Form* as appropriate. These forms can be found on our internet home page.

1. From the Court internet home page, select *Attorney Info.*
2. Select *Sacramento.*
3. Scroll down and select *Forms.*
4. Select *Civil Forms.*
5. Scroll down and click on *Appeal Transcript Designation and Order Form or Electronic Court Reporter Transcript Order Form.*

Completed forms should be submitted to Jonathan Anderson, (916) 930-4072, janderson@caed.uscourts.gov

AUDIO/VISUAL EQUIPMENT: The Sacramento Clerk's office has a variety of audio/visual equipment available to use for trial purposes. Available equipment may include: ELMOs, projectors, plasma screens, TVs and VCRs. In order to learn about the equipment provided by the court, you can access our internet home page and follow these procedures:

 1. From the Court internet home page, select *Attorney Info Tab*.
 2. Select *Sacramento*.
 3. Scroll down and select *Electronic Courtroom*.
 4. Select *Audio Systems or Video Systems* as applicable.

Attorneys should arrange, through the Courtroom Deputy, a time to meet with court Information Technology staff for training on electronic equipment. Appointments should be scheduled at least one to two weeks prior to trial.

COURTROOM DEPUTY: If you have any questions or need further information, please contact Kyle Owen at (916) 930-4004 or kowen@caed.uscourts.gov .

Hon. Dale A. Drozd
Chief Magistrate Judge

Chambers Information
U.S. District Court, Eastern District of California
Courtroom No. 27, 8th Floor
501 I Street
Sacramento, CA 95814

Scheduling Information
Courtroom Deputy: (916) 930-4128

Civil Law and Motion	Fridays at 10:00 a.m.
Criminal Law and Motion	Tuesdays at 10:00 a.m.
Jury Trials	Mondays at 10:00 a.m.
Court Trials	Wednesdays at 9:00 a.m.

Biographical Information
Federal Judicial Service:
- U.S. District Court, Eastern District of California
- Appointed as United States Magistrate Judge, 1997.

Education:
- University of Southern California, 1973 - 1975
- California State University, San Diego, B.A. 1977
- University of California, Los Angeles, J.D., 1980

Professional Career:
- Law Clerk for U.S. District Judge Lawrence K. Karlton, Eastern District of CA, 1980-1982
- Private Practice, San Francisco, CA, 1982-1985
- Private Practice, Sacramento, CA, 1986-1997

I.   **Judge Drozd's Procedures and Practices**

Civil Law and Motion
Civil law and motion is heard every Friday at 10:00 a.m.

DATES ARE NOT RESERVERD. File moving papers in accordance with the Local and Federal Rules.

Parties interested in appearing by telephone are to contact Pete Buzo 48-hours before a scheduled hearing.

Criminal Law and Motion
Criminal law and motion is heard every Tuesday at 10:00 a.m.

DATES ARE NOT RESERVERD. File moving papers in accordance with the Local and Federal Rules.

Jury Trials
Jury Trials set on Mondays at 10:00 a.m. Dark on Fridays.

Court Trials
Court Trials are heard on Wednesdays at 9:00 a.m.

*****SETTLEMENT CONFERENCES: AS SET BY
COURTROOM DEPUTY*****

Hon. Gregory G. Hollows
Magistrate Judge

Chambers Information
U.S. District Court, Eastern District of California
Courtroom No. 9, 13th Floor
501 I Street
Sacramento, CA 95814

Scheduling Information
Courtroom Deputy: (916) 930-4199

Biographical Information
Federal Judicial Service:
- U. S. District Court, Eastern District of California
- Appointed as United States Magistrate Judge, March 7, 1990. Served as chief judge, 1997-2002.

Education:
- Muskingum College, B.A., 1969
- Loyola Law School, J.D., *magna cum laude* 1979

Professional Career:
- Private Practice, Los Angeles, San Jose, CA, 1979-1982
- Deputy Chief U.S. Attorney, Eastern District of California, 1982-1988
- Chief, Civil Division, U.S. Attorney's Office, Eastern District of California, 1988-1990

I.   **Judge Hollows' Procedures and Practices**
         Civil Law and Motion Calendars are held on Thursdays at 10:00 a.m. Please Call
         (916) 930-4199 for the latest updated information concerning scheduling of matters.

Hon. Craig M. Kellison
Magistrate Judge

Chambers Information
U.S. District Court, Eastern District of California
Courtroom No. 304, 3rd Floor
2986 Bechelli Lane
Redding, CA 96002

Scheduling Information
Courtroom Deputy: (530) 246-5416

Biographical Information
Federal Judicial Service:
- United States District Court Eastern District of California
- Appointed as United States Magistrate Judge (part-time), November 1, 1988.
- Appointed as United States Magistrate Judge (full-time), September 2, 2004.

Education:
- University of Nevada - Reno, B.S., 1968-1972
- Gonzaga Universtiy School of Law, J.D., 1973-1976

Professional Career:
- Law Clerk, Hon. Bruce R. Thompson, United States District Court, District of Nevada, 1976-1978
- Private Practice, Susanville, CA, 1978-2004
- Administrative Law Judge, *pro tem*, State of California, 2000-2004

Hon. Barbara A. McAuliffe
Magistrate Judge

Chambers Information
U.S. District Court, Eastern District of California
Courtroom No. 8, 6th Floor
2500 Tulare Street
Fresno, CA 93721

Scheduling Information
Courtroom Deputy: (559) 499-5788

Civil Law and Motion	Fridays at 9:00 a.m.

Biographical Information
Federal Judicial Service:
- United States District Court, Eastern District of California
- Appointed as United States Magistrate Judge on October 14, 2011

Education:
- Louisiana State University, B.S., 1980
- University of San Diego School of Law, J.D., 1989; Executive Editor of the Law Review; *Magna Cum Laude*

Professional Career:
- Gibson, Dunn & Crutcher, Los Angeles, CA, 1989-1991
- Lang, Richert & Patch, Fresno, CA, 1991-1995
- Partner, Motschiedler, Michaelides & Wishon, Fresno, CA, 1995 to 2000
- Law Clerk, Chambers of Judge Lawrence J. O'Neill, 2000-2011

I. Judge McAuliffe's Procedures and Practices

1. Civil Law and Motion Calendar:

a) Judge McAuliffe does NOT issue tentative rulings.

b) Hearings are on Fridays at 9:00 a.m. in Courtroom #8 - motion dates are not reserved.

c) Parties do not need to clear a motion hearing date. File your moving papers in accordance with the Local and Federal Rules, if the date conflicts with the Court's calendar, the Court will reschedule the matter by minute order. DATES ARE NOT RESERVED.

d) Paper copies of all motion-related documents, properly tabbed, fastened, and clearly identified as a "Courtesy Copy" shall be submitted to the court, Attention: Judge McAuliffe.

e) On short notice, Minute Orders may be issued vacating the hearing and taking the matter under submission pursuant to Local Rule 230(g) (Fed. R. Civ. P. 78) - *please refer to the court's Notice of Electronic Filing.*

f) Motion dates are subject to change at the court's discretion.

2. Scheduling Conferences:

A JOINT Scheduling Conference Report, carefully prepared and executed by all counsel, shall be electronically filed in full compliance with the requirements set forth in the Order Setting Mandatory Scheduling Conference, one (1) full week prior to the Scheduling Conference, and a copy shall be e-mailed, in WordPerfect or Word format, to bamorders@caed.uscourts.gov.

3. Settlement Conferences:

a) The case must be ready for meaningful settlement discussions. Plaintiff must make a demand to defendants and initial settlement negotiations must take place prior to the Settlement Conference being held.

b) *Confidential* Settlement Conference Statements are **MANDATORY** from each party, and must be submitted to Judge McAuliffe's chambers **at least seven (7) calendar days prior to the Settlement Conference**.

c) Parties must appear with counsel.

d) Upon written request with *good cause* submitted for Judge McAuliffe's approval, some telephonic appearances may be granted.

4. Telephonic Appearances:

a) Telephonic appearances by local or out-of-town counsel are encouraged.

b) Please notify the courtroom deputy if one or more attorneys will be appearing telephonically, so that a notation can be placed on the court calendar.

c) Counsel shall make arrangements for and shall initiate the conference call at the scheduled time.

d) *After all parties are on the line*, the call should be placed to Judge McAuliffe's chambers at 559-499-5789.

5. **Discovery Hearings:**
Local Rule 251(a) (Fed.R.Civi.P. 37) requires a joint statement. <u>However, with the press of business, Judge McAuliffe **REQUIRES** a joint statement re discovery disagreement be filed seven (7) days before the scheduled hearing date (i.e., the Friday before the customary Friday hearing)</u>. Any motion will be dropped from calendar if the statement is not timely filed, and courtesy copies of all motion-related documents, including the 251 statement, declarations, and exhibits (see #1d above), are not delivered to the Clerk's Office by 9:00 a.m. on the fourth (4th) day (Monday) prior to the hearing (customarily on Friday).

6. **Informal Telephonic Conferences re Discovery Disputes:**
a) If the parties stipulate, Judge McAuliffe will resolve discovery disputes outside the formal Local Rule 251 procedures.

b) After obtaining the available dates and times from the courtroom deputy and agreeing upon a date and time with opposing counsel, confirm with the courtroom deputy when the parties will be calling in. All parties must appear telephonically.

c) At least 24 hours before the conference, the parties should fax or email to chambers a two-page synopsis (no exhibits or attachments) of their dispute. Fax: 559-494-3920 and/or Email: bamorders@caed.uscourts.gov.

7. **All Documents Requiring Court Approval:**
As required by Local Rule 137(b), counsel shall submit all proposed orders, stipulations, etc., in either Word Perfect (preferred) or Miscrosoft Word format, to chambers at bamorders@caed.uscourts.gov. Pursuant to Local Rule 131(c), the documents should include the attorneys' electronic signatures (i.e., <u>/s/First/Last name</u>), as well as the date the document was signed.

8. **Length of Briefs on Motions other than Rule 251 motions:**
Unless prior leave of Court is obtained seven days before the filing date, all moving and opposition briefs or legal memorandum in civil cases shall not exceed 25 pages. Reply briefs filed by moving parties shall not exceed 10 pages. Any brief exceeding 10 pages shall include a table of contents and a table of authorities. Briefs that exceed the page limitations or are sought to be filed without leave may not be considered. If combined supporting papers or opposition papers exceed 25 pages, the parties are required to submit <u>a complete set</u> of all papers as chambers courtesy copy, properly tabbed and fastened.

Hon. John F. Moulds
Magistrate Judge

Chambers Information
U.S. District Court, Eastern District of California
Courtroom: 8th Floor
501 I Street
Sacramento, CA 95814

Scheduling Information
Courtroom Deputy: (916) 930-4072

Civil Law and Motion	Thursdays at 11:00 a.m.

Biographical Information
Federal Judicial Service:
- U. S. District Court, Eastern District of California
- Appointed as United States Magistrate Judge, 1986. Served as Chief Magistrate Judge, 1987-1997. Part-time U.S. Magistrate Judge, Eastern District of California, January 1983 to December 1985.

Education:
- Stanford University, 1955-1958
- California State University, Sacramento, B.A. with honors, 1960
- University of California Berkeley, Boalt Hall School of Law, J.D., 1966

Professional Career:
- Research Analyst, CA State Senate Fact-Finding Committee on Education, 1960-1961
- Administrative Assistant, California State Senator Albert S. Rodda, 1961-1963
- Legal Editor, California Continuing Education of the Bar, 1964-1966
- California Rural Legal Assistance, Staff Attorney, 1966-1968
- Sacramento Legal Aid, Staff Attorney, 1968
- California Rural Legal Assistance, Directing Attorney, Marysville Field Office & Sacramento Legislative Advocacy Office, 1968-1969
- Private Practice, Sacramento, CA, 1969-1985

Professional Organizations:
- President, Federal Magistrate Judges Association, 1992-1993; Officer & Director, 1988-1992

I.   **Judge Moulds' Procedures and Practices**

CIVIL LAW AND MOTION:

Civil law and motion is heard every Thursday at 11:00 a.m.

MOTION DATES ARE NOT RESERVED. Simply file your moving papers in accordance with the Local and Federal Rules.

Parties interested in appearing by telephone must contact Jonathan Anderson.

TRANSCRIPT ORDERS:

If you wish to order a transcript for a hearing held before Magistrate Judge John F. Moulds (or another Magistrate Judge in the Eastern District-Sacramento Division), you will need to complete the *Electronic Court Reporter Transcript Order Form* or the *Appeal Transcript Designation and Order Form* as appropriate. These forms can be found on our internet home page.

1) From the Court intranet home page, select *Attorney Info Tab*

2) Scroll down and click on the link to *Forms*

3) Click on *Civil Forms*

4) Scroll down and click on *Appeal Transcript Designation and Order Form or Electronic Court Reporter Transcript Order Form*

Completed forms should be submitted to Jonathan Anderson.

Hon. Kendall J. Newman
Magistrate Judge

Chambers Information

U.S. District Court, Eastern District of California
Courtroom No. 25, 8th Floor
501 I Street
Sacramento, CA 95814

Scheduling Information

Courtroom Deputy: (916) 930-4187

Civil Law and Motion	Thursdays at 10:00 a.m.
Criminal Law and Motion	Wednesdays at 9:00 a.m. (Non-Duty Calendar) Wednesdays at 2:00 p.m. ("Duty" Calendar)

Biographical Information

Federal Judicial Service:

- U.S. District Court, Eastern District of California
- Appointed as United States Magistrate Judge, February 8, 2010

Education:

- Cornell University, B.S., 1980
- College of William and Mary, J.D., 1984

Professional Career:

- Private Practice, San Diego, CA, 1984-1990
- U.S. Attorney's Office, Southern District of California, 1990-1994
- U.S. Attorney's Office, Eastern District of California, 1995-2010

I. **Judge Newman's Procedures and Practices**

CRIMINAL LAW AND MOTION: Criminal law and motion is heard every Wednesday at 9:00 a.m. except when Judge Newman is "Duty," then his criminal law and motion calendar is held on any "Duty" Calendar at 2:00 PM.

CIVIL LAW AND MOTION: Civil law and motion is heard every Thursday at 10:00 a.m. **MOTION DATES ARE NOT RESERVED.** Simply file your moving papers in accordance with the Local and Federal Rules.

Telephonic Appearance: Parties interested in appearing by telephone must file a request and proposed order.

Proposed Orders: As required by the local rules, counsel shall submit via email, to kjnorders@caed.uscourts.gov, the proposed order accompanying any application, request, stipulation or motion in either Word Perfect (preferred) or Microsoft Word format. Pursuant to Local Rule 131 (c), the document should include the attorneys' electronic signature(s) (i.e., /s/ First/Last name), as well as the date the document was signed.

TRANSCRIPT ORDERS: If you wish to order a transcript for a hearing held before Magistrate Judge Kendall J. Newman (or another Magistrate Judge in the Eastern District-Sacramento Division), you will need to complete the *Electronic Court Reporter Transcript Order Form* or the *Appeal Transcript Designation and Order Form* as appropriate. These forms can be found on our internet home page.

> 1. From the Court internet home page, select *Attorney Info.*
>
> 2. Select *Sacramento.*
>
> 3. Scroll down and select *Forms.*
>
> 4. Select *Civil Forms.*
>
> 5. Scroll down and click on *Appeal Transcript Designation and Order Form* or *Electronic Court Reporter Transcript Order Form*

Completed forms should be submitted to Jonathan Anderson, (916) 930-4072 or janderson@caed.uscourts.gov

AUDIO/VISUAL EQUIPMENT: The Sacramento Clerk's office has a variety of audio/visual equipment available to use for trial purposes. Available equipment may include: ELMOs, projectors, plasma screens, TVs and VCRs. In order to learn about the equipment provided by the court, you can access our internet home page and follow these procedures:

> 1. From the Court internet home page, select *Attorney Info Tab.*
>
> 2. Select *Sacramento.*
>
> 3. Scroll down and select *Electronic Courtroom.*
>
> 4. Select *Audio Systems* or *Video Systems* as applicable.

Attorneys should arrange, through the Courtroom Deputy, a time to meet with court Information Technology staff for training on electronic equipment. Appointments should be scheduled at least one to two weeks prior to trial.

COURTROOM DEPUTY: If you have any questions or need further information, please contact Matt Caspar (916) 930-4187 or mcaspar@caed.uscourts.gov.

Hon. Sheila K. Oberto
Magistrate Judge

Chambers Information
U.S. District Court, Eastern District of California
Courtroom No. 7, 6th Floor
2500 Tulare Street
Fresno, CA 93721

Scheduling Information
Courtroom Deputy: (559) 499-5975

Biographical Information
Federal Judicial Service:
- U.S. District Court, Eastern District of California
- Appointed United States Magistrate Judge on April 12, 2010

Education:
- University of Southern California, B.S., 1977
- UCLA, M.S., 1979
- University of Southern California School of Law, J.D., 1985

Professional Career:
- Law Clerk, Justice Armand Arabian, California Court of Appeals, Second Appellate District, 1985-87
- Private Practice, Irell & Manella, Los Angeles, CA, 1988-89
- Private Practice, Baker, Manock & Jensen, Fresno, CA, 1990-99
- Assistant United States Attorney, Civil Division, Eastern District of California, Fresno, CA 1999-2010
- Assistant United States Attorney, Criminal Division, Eastern District of California, Fresno, CA, 1/2006 – 1/2008, Deputy Chief, Fresno Office; 2/2008 – 4/9/2010, Chief, White Collar Crime Unit

Hon. Michael J. Seng
Magistrate Judge

Chambers Information
U.S. District Court, Eastern District of California
9004 Castle Cliffs Court
Yosemite, CA 95389

Scheduling Information
Courtroom Deputy: (209) 372-0320

Civil Law and Motion	Second and fourth Friday of every month at 9:30 a.m.
Settlement Conferences	Second and fourth Thursday of every month
Criminal Law and Motion	Daily (as necessary) at 1:30 p.m.

Biographical Information
Federal Judicial Service:
- U. S. District Court, Eastern District of California
- Appointed United States Magistrate Judge on April 2, 2010

Education:
- University of Tennessee School of Business, B.A., 1969
- University of Tennessee College of Law, J.D., 1975

Professional Career:
- United States Army, 1971-1973
- Staff Attorney, U.S. DHEW, SSA, OHA, Fresno, CA, 1975-1978
- Civil Litigation (attorney/partner/director), Blumberg, Sherr & Kerkorian (and its successors); Farley, Seng, DeSantos & Green; and Seng & Stratton, Fresno, CA, 1978-2008
- U.S. Administrative Law Judge, Office of Disability Adjudication and Review, Sacramento, 2008-2010

I.   **Judge Seng's Procedures and Practices**

I.   **GENERAL INFORMATION**

A. Filing. No civil filings are accepted in Yosemite. We are supported by the Fresno Division of the Clerk's Office. Please contact them at (559) 499-5600.

B. Telephonic appearances. Parties may appear telephonically by making reservations through Court Call at 866-582-6878. Please send confirmations of reservations (and/or questions) to mjsorders@caed.uscourts.gov and lyu@caed.uscourts.gov.

C. Documents Requiring Court Approval. As required by Local Rule, counsel shall submit via email to mjsorders@caed.uscourts.gov all proposed orders, applications, requests, stipulations, etc., in either Word Perfect (preferred) or Microsoft Word format. Pursuant to Local Rule 131(a)(c), the document should include the attorney(s) electronic signature(s) (i.e., /s/ First Last name), as well as the date the document was signed.

II.   **CIVIL CASES**

A. Motion hearings. Matters are heard at 9:30 p.m. on the 2nd and 4th Friday of every month in Courtroom # 6 of the Fresno courthouse. Dates DO NOT need to be cleared in advance with the Court. Moving papers are to be filed in accordance with the Local and Federal Rules. If the date chosen by the filing party conflicts with the Courtâ€™s calendar, the Court will reschedule the matter by minute order. Motion dates may not be reserved.

B. Discovery motions. No written discovery motion may be noticed or set for hearing before Magistrate Judge Michael J. Seng without his prior approval.

A party with a discovery dispute shall confer with the opposing party in a good faith effort to resolve the dispute without court action. If such effort fails, the moving party shall, prior to filing a notice of motion, email to MJSorders @caed.uscourts.gov a request for a pre-motion telephone conference with the Magistrate Judge. The request shall be deemed to include a professional representation by the requesting lawyer that a good faith effort to resolve the dispute took place but failed, and it shall advise the Court of dates and times in the next ten day period when any concerned party cannot be available to confer regarding the dispute.

Upon emailing the request, the moving party shall contact the Court's Career Law Clerk at the number provided above and advise of the issues in dispute.

The Court will issue a minute order advising counsel of the time and date of the telephone conference. The parties shall make reservations to appear through Court Call. No recording of the conference shall take place except with prior permission of the Court. No papers shall be filed or lodged in connection with the conference unless the Career Clerk determines that same are necessary to enable the Magistrate Judge to resolve the dispute.

If the Magistrate Judge decides that motion papers and supporting memoranda are needed to satisfactorily resolve the dispute, he shall approve the filing of a written motion filed in conformity with Local Rule 251(a). (The provisions of local Rule 251 (b) through (f) will not apply unless the Magistrate Judge so orders.) Such motion shall, without limitation, (1) quote in full each interrogatory, deposition question, request for admission, or request for production in dispute and (2) the response or objection and grounds therefor as stated by the opposing party.

Unless otherwise ordered by the Court, deposition transcripts or discovery papers shall not be lodged or filed with the Court.

C. Settlement Conferences. Settlement Conferences

C. Settlement Conferences. Settlement Conferences will be scheduled on the 2nd and 4th Thursday of each month in Courtroom 6 of the Fresno Courthouse. Parties must appear with counsel, unless otherwise ordered. Telephonic appearances are discouraged but may be considered. A written request with cause must be forwarded to Judge Seng for approval. Each party must submit a settlement conference statement to Judge Seng's Yosemite chambers at least seven (7) calendar days prior to the Settlement Conference. Electronic versions may be emailed to mjsorders@caed.uscourts.gov.

D. Scheduling Conferences. A Joint Scheduling Conference Report carefully prepared and executed by all counsel, shall be electronically filed in CM/ECF in full compliance with the requirements set forth in the previously served ORDER SETTING MANDATORY SCHEDULING CONFERENCE at least one (1) full week prior to the Scheduling Conference, and shall be emailed, in WordPerfect or Word format, to mjsorders@caed.uscourts.gov.

III.   **CRIMINAL MOTIONS AND HEARINGS**
A. Hearings. Criminal hearings are set daily (as necessary) at 1:30 p.m. The hearing location is 9004 Castle Cliff Court. Contact Laurie C. Yu to set criminal matters, as pertinent information must be attained relative to interpreters, court appointed counsel, pretrial services, probation, U.S. Marshals and/or any other Federal Law Enforcement agency.

IV.   **CENTRAL VIOLATIONS BUREAU (CVB) VIOLATION NOTICES.**
If you were referred to chambers to speak with Laurie C. Yu regarding a violation involving the Central Violations Bureau, please email her at lyu@caed.uscourts.gov .

FREQUENTLY ASKED QUESTIONS RE: CVB MATTERS
A. Payments. Payments are not accepted in Court or at the Yosemite Courthouse. You can either mail your payments to CVB, or make a payment on the CVB website at www.cvb.uscourts.gov using a credit or debit card, or a checking account. If you are seeking an extension with respect to a Court ordered fine, please be advised that NO EXTENSIONS are granted. If you

miss your deadline, you risk late penalties and referral to a collection agency. Please contact CVB directly to ascertain late fees, etc., at 1-800-827-2982.

B. Traffic School. All moving violations are reported to the Department of Motor Vehicles regardless of state. You may request traffic school by submitting a written request that includes violation number, name and an self addressed, stamped envelope to:

The Central Violations Bureau Clerk
P.O. Box 575
Yosemite National Park, 95389

Please note, it may take a 4 to 6 weeks to receive a reply, DO NOT PAY YOUR TICKET before receiving traffic school instructions.

C. Abstracts/Arrest Warrants. If the Court has issued an arrest warrant or filed an abstract against you, your only remedy is to pay your fine or request a new court date. Your abstract or arrest warrant will NOT be released UNTIL all monetary penalties and fines imposed on you are PAID IN FULL.

D. Appearances in Court. If you are unable to appear before the Court on the date stated on your violation, you can request in writing that the Court assign you a new court date. Be advised that the U.S. Magistrate Court in Yosemite hears CVB matters on Tuesdays at 1:00 p.m. Please include in your written request the original court date and the date to which you wish your case to be moved. The new court date must be on a Tuesday no more than 30 days from the original court date. Requests may be faxed to (209) 372-0324 or emailed to lyu@caed.uscourts.gov.

Hon. Sandra M. Snyder
Magistrate Judge

Chambers Information
U.S. District Court, Eastern District of California
Courtroom No. 1, 8th Floor
2500 Tulare Street
Fresno, CA 93721

Scheduling Information
Courtroom Deputy: (559) 499-5690

Civil Law and Motion	Wednesdays at 10:00 a.m.

Biographical Information
Federal Judicial Service:
- U. S. District Court, Eastern District of California
- Appointed as United States Magistrate Judge, May 3, 1993.

Education:
- California State University, Fresno, B.A. English, 1968
- Golden Gate University, School of Law, San Francisco, J.D., 1976

Professional Career:
- Assistant to the Dean, Golden Gate Univ. School of Law, San Francisco, 1970-1973
- Private Practice, Porterville, CA, 1977-1978
- Assistant Director of Development, Golden Gate Univ. School of Law, 1979-1980
- Deputy District Attorney, Fresno, CA, 1980-1981
- Private Practice, Fresno, CA, 1981-1989
- Judge, Fresno County Municipal Court, 1989-1991
- Judge, Fresno County Superior Court, 1991-1993

I. **Judge Snyder's Procedures and Practices**

1. **Civil Law and Motion Calendar**

a) Judge Snyder does NOT issue tentative rulings.

b) Hearings are customarily on Wednesdays at 10:00 a.m. in Courtroom No. 1; motion dates are not reserved, and the matter will be placed on the Court's Calendar only after the motion is filed.

c) Counsel must first call chambers at 559-499-5690 to clear a date for a motion hearing.

d) Paper copies of all motion-related documents, exceeding 50 pages pursuant to Local Rule 133(f), properly tabbed, fastened, and clearly identified as a "Courtesy Copy" shall be submitted to the court, Attention: Judge Snyder.

e) On short notice, Minute Orders may be issued vacating the hearing and taking the matter under submission pursuant to Local Rule 230(g) (Fed. R. Civ. P. 78) - please refer to the court's Notice of Electronic Filing.

f) Motion dates are subject to change at the Court's discretion.

2. **Scheduling Conferences**

A JOINT Scheduling Report, carefully prepared and executed by all counsel, shall be electronically filed in full compliance with the specific requirements set forth in Exhibit "A" attached to the (initial) Order Setting Mandatory Scheduling Conference, one (1) full week prior to the Scheduling Conference, and a copy shall be e-mailed, in WordPerfect or Word format, to smsorders@caed.uscourts.gov.

3. **Settlement Conferences**

a) Plaintiff must provide a demand to defendants; initial settlement negotiations must take place prior to the Settlement Conference, and defendants must have settlement authority - not just nuisance value.

b) *Confidential* Settlement Conference Statements are **MANDATORY** from each party, and must be submitted directly to Judge Snyder's chambers **at least seven (7) calendar days prior to the Settlement Conference**.

c) Parties must personally appear with counsel who will try the case.

d) Upon written request, with good cause submitted for Judge Snyder(s) approval, some telephonic appearances may be granted.

4. **Telephonic Appearances**

a) Telephonic appearances by out-of-town counsel are always and strongly encouraged.

b) Please notify the courtroom deputy if one or more attorneys will be appearing telephonically so that a notation can be made on the court calendar.

c) Counsel shall make arrangements for and initiate the single conference call at the scheduled time.

d) *After all parties are on the line*, the call should then be placed to Judge Snyder's chambers at 559-499-5690.

5. **Telephonic Conferences re Discovery Disputes**

a) After obtaining the available dates and times from the courtroom deputy, and agreeing upon a date and time with opposing counsel, confirm with the courtroom deputy when the parties will be calling in. All parties must appear telephonically.

b) 24 hours prior to the conference, a[n optional - depending on the depth and breadth of the dispute] **two-page** synopsis (no exhibits or attachments allowed) may be faxed by each counsel to chambers at 559-499-5926.

6. **Discovery Hearings**

Local Rule 251(a) (Fed.R.Civi.P. 37) requires a joint statement. However, with the press of business, Judge Snyder **REQUIRES** that a joint statement re discovery disagreement be filed seven (7) days prior to the scheduled hearing date (i.e., the Wednesday before the customary Wednesday hearing). Any motion will be dropped from calendar if the statement is not timely filed, and courtesy copies of all motion-related documents, including the 251 stipulation, declarations, and exhibits (see #1d above), are not delivered to the Clerk's Office by 9:00 a.m. on the Wednesday prior to the customary hearing on Wednesday.

7. **All Documents Requiring Court Approval**

As required by Local Rule 137(b), counsel shall submit mail to: smsorders@caed.uscourts.gov all proposed orders, stipulations, etc., in either Word Perfect (preferred) or Miscrosoft Word format, to chambers at smsorders@caed.uscourts.gov. Pursuant to Local Rule 131(c), the documents should include the attorneys electronic signatures (i.e., **/s/First/Last name**), as well as the date the document was signed.

Hon. Jennifer L. Thurston
Magistrate Judge

Chambers Information
U.S. District Court, Eastern District of California
First Floor (U.S. Bankruptcy Courtroom)
1300 18th Street
Bakersfield, CA 93301

Scheduling Information
Courtroom Deputy: (661) 326-6620

Civil Law and Motion	- Mondays at 9:00 a.m. (for cases venued outside of Kern County); - Tuesdays through Thursdays at 9:00 a.m. (for cases venued in Kern County)
Scheduling Conferences and Settlement Conferences	Wednesdays and Thursdays at 9:00 a.m.
Criminal Law and Motion	Daily (as necessary) at 2:30 p.m.

Biographical Information
[Not available]

I.   **Judge Thurston's Procedures and Practices**

CIVIL MATTERS

Civil law and motion is heard [on these days] at 9:00 a.m. Utilize the locations listed below for your Notice of Motions as follows:

> Cases venued **in Kern County**: **1300 18th Street, Bakersfield** (Bankruptcy Courtroom) are heard on Tuesdays through Thursdays.

> Cases venued **outside Kern County**: **Courtroom 6, Fresno**, U.S. District Court are heard on Mondays.

Dates DO NOT need to be cleared with the Court. File your moving papers in accordance with the Local and Federal Rules, if the date conflicts with the Court's calendar, the Court will reschedule the matter by minute order. DATES ARE NOT RESERVED.

Scheduling Conferences and Settlement conferences are normally heard on Wednesdays and Thursdays starting at 9:00 a.m. Conference hearing locations are as follows:

> Cases venued **in Kern County**: **1200 Truxtun Avenue, Suite 120**, Bakersfield (Chambers).

> Cases venued outside Kern County: **Courtroom 6, Fresno**, U.S. District Court.

No filings are accepted in Bakersfield. We are supported by the Fresno Division, Clerk's Office. Please contact them at (559) 499-5600.

TELEPHONIC APPEARANCES - parties may appear telephonically by making reservations through Court Call at 866-582-6878. Submit confirmation of your reservations to jltorders@caed.uscourts.gov and aleon-guerrero@caed.uscourts.gov .

CHAMBERS COURTESY PAPER COPIES - Chambers is located in Bakersfield. Do not mail courtesy copies to the Fresno Division. Courtesy copies should be mailed to: 1200 Truxtun Avenue, Suite 120, Bakersfield, CA 93301. (*For further information refer to Local Rule 133(f)*)

CRIMINAL MATTERS

Criminal hearings are set daily (as necessary) at 2:30 p.m. The hearing location is **1300 18th Street**. Contact Alan Leon-Guerrero to set criminal matters ASAP, as pertinent information must be attained relative to interpreters, court appointed counsel, pretrial services, probation, U.S. Marshals and/or any other Federal Law Enforcement agency.

Central Violations Bureau (CVB) violation notices: If you were referred to chambers to speak with Alan Leon-Guerrero, please email him at aleon-guerrero@caed.uscourts.gov, or see frequently asked questions below.

FREQUENTLY ASKED QUESTIONS

Payments: Payments are not accepted in Court. You must mail your payments to

CVB, or made on the CVB website at www.cvb.uscourts.gov with credit, debit or checking account. If you are seeking an extension from a Court ordered fine, please be advised that **NO EXTENSIONS** are granted. As well, you risk late penalties and referral to a collection agency. Contact CVB to ascertain late fees, etc., at 1-800-827-2982.

Traffic School: You may attend traffic school without making an appearance in Court. Send an email requesting to attend traffic school to: aleon-guerrero@caed.uscourts.gov, or call 661-326-6624.

Abstracts/Arrest Warrants: Pay your fine or **request a new court date**. Your abstract or arrest warrant will NOT be released UNTIL all monetary penalties and fines imposed on you are PAID IN FULL.

New Court date: You must contact the agency that cited you, and stipulate to a new court date. The agency you must contact is identified on the top right corner of your violation notice, entitled **CVB location code**, contact that prosecutor of that location code at one the following below:

CVB location code	Place of Offense	Prosecutor	Contact Info
CA14/CA3F	Edwards AFB	S. Small	(661) 277-4380, (661) 277-2888 afftc.ja.generallaw@edwards.af.mil
CA20	BLM (Bishop)	E. Keefer	(760) 872-5016 Eric_Keefer@blm.gov
CA24	BLM (Ridgecrest)	T. Allen	(760) 384-5466 tmallen@blm.ca.gov
CA26	BLM (Bakersfield)	B. Chartier	(661) 391-6000 Brien_Chartier@blm.gov
CA32	USFS (Bishop)	R. Watt	(760) 873-2520 rwatt@fs.fed.us
CA35/CA40	USFS (Bakersfield)	J. Norris	(760) 376-3781 x-618 jnorris@fs.fed.us
CA71	NPS (Death Valley)	M. Natrass	(760) 786-3291 Mike_Nattrass@nps.gov

www.ingramcontent.com/pod-product-compliance
Lightning Source LLC
Chambersburg PA
CBHW081551220326
41598CB00036B/6637